a child's eye view

a child's eye view

Piaget for young parents and teachers

Mary Sime

(Principal Lecturer in Education, Chorley College of Education)

supported by a team of her colleagues and students

with 97 illustrations and 30 line drawings

Thames and Hudson · London

All photographs were taken by the author, except that on page 85.

Printed and bound in Great Britain by Jarrold and Sons Ltd, Norwich

ISBN 0 500 01094 3

CONTENTS

PREFACE

Several valuable attempts have been made at simplifying (M. Brearley) and at condensing (N. Isaacs) the works of Professor Jean Piaget, in an effort to make them more readily available than they used to be for students of colleges of education. This is NO SUCH FURTHER ATTEMPT.

This small book aims at *enlivening* a few of the key points of Piaget's theories and at whetting the appetite for more. It aims at bringing some of the results of his research to students who are training for teachers and also to the ever-increasing number of young parents who, in this generation, are wanting to take a scientific interest in the developmental psychology of their own young children. The parents may want to read nothing more concentrated than this book: it is hoped that the students will find that this book introduces them to the spirit of Piaget sufficiently well to encourage them to turn to the intellectually 'heavy' reading of the direct translations of Piaget's own books and that they will, as a result of their reading, turn to experimentation somewhat of the nature that is described here.

The examples of activities presented in this book are *not* valid as clinical evidence. The examples described in Piaget's own books *are*, of course, clinically valid. Our tests were not administered in clinical conditions for two reasons:

1   For one thing, the short time allotted to 'Education' in a college of education would make it impossible for any student to repeat, clinically, more than a very few of Piaget's actual tests: any statistics thus obtained would, therefore, be too few to be other than tentative illustrations of the behaviour Piaget describes.

7

2   It takes more experience than can be gained in a three-year college course to enable a student to probe beneath a child's immediate and superficial response, by posing quick, yet carefully conceived, supplementary questions adequate for clinical validity. But he can, with perseverance, get very near to such validity.

These two difficulties lead many tutors to refrain from encouraging Piagetian testing. But Piagetian books are doubly difficult to read (and to believe!) unless students, from the beginning of their first college year, see live examples of the responses on which Piaget based his theories. The two drawbacks mentioned above are strongly counterbalanced by the tendency of children frequently *spontaneously* to express their thoughts in play and in the problematic situations that they meet in the activity learning of the primary classrooms today. The teacher needs to be alert to register these illustrative remarks and statements of conviction that are ejaculated in random order. A teacher also needs to be able to probe a child's understanding by posing a problem (and providing materials for its solution) in the way that Piaget has taught us to do. Hence practice in setting Piagetian diagnostic tests, and in skilfully questioning to find a child's genuine thoughts on a subject, are a necessary part of the training of a modern teacher. Equally necessary is experience in listening critically, with Piagetian interpretation in mind, to the corporate opinions of genuinely interested small children as they argue out the solution of a problem with one another and so reveal to the listening adult their stages of security or insecurity in concept formations, their stages in the development of reasoning techniques, their stages in maturity of moral judgment and their stages of progress towards the formal thinking of adolescence and adulthood. Only by keeping an eye on these developments can a teacher know how and when to provide the rightly enriched environment and the carefully posed problems that will keep the child making steady and happy progress.
While of no value to the research worker, such illustrations are just what the training college student will benefit from, by observing them and by trying to precipitate them, not only in his college days but also throughout his teaching career.
It was teachers who lacked this ability, in the past, that built for many of today's adults a blurred horror, wrongly called 'mathematics', that is merely an edifice on a false foundation. Such faulty teaching made some of us hate what we think to be mathematics: it has made others fight shy of writing; it has made many classify themselves as inartistic or unmusical. The good

student of Piaget will guard against any such faulty foundation. He will also enjoy his teaching career the more if he understands the developmental psychology of the children he is teaching. And, in the same way, parents will enjoy helping their children mature in intellectual growth.

Students at Chorley College were encouraged to adapt some of Piaget's tests to their own purposes, mostly in non-clinical conditions, and to observe children's reactions at different ages as they discussed with their own peers the problems involved. In this sort of social setting students joined in with the discussions (thus getting in supplementary questioning) whenever they considered that they could do so as welcome friends rather than as testing adults. In this way they saw ample examples to vivify their own reading. They also found plentiful examples in which children's thoughts were not clarified: this lack of clarity was, in fact, enlightening to the students and it sparked off discussion among them and drove them to an even more critical reading of Piaget's own examples.

It would be impossible in such a short report as this to aim at covering, even thinly, the work undertaken in this way by the students: certainly, one could not even *introduce* the great breadth of Piaget's work. Nor have any parts of the work been covered in great depth. What has seemed of more value to us is the highlighting, through illustrated examples, of the structural framework of mental growth that Piaget has guided us to expect to find. An understanding of these key points guided the thinking of the students in their group teaching practices and a few examples of the resultant teaching are also quoted in Appendices I and II.

Examples from this work have been gathered together as the chapters of this book. Some of the students, mature men and women who had previously held responsible posts in careers other than teaching, took part in actually producing Chapters Two, Four, Seven, Eight, Ten and Eleven and their names are shown at the appropriate points. They also helped in other parts of the team effort. The whole team was very large — too numerous in membership for names to be recorded, but many of their own children are recorded here in photographic form. Other photographs in the book are almost all of children of tutorial and clerical staff and of domestic staff of the College. Just a very few photographs were taken in Lancashire schools and two only are of the children of a personal friend, unconnected with college life.

To all these children, of students and of staff and of friends, and to the few children from the schools, we offer our gratitude for their continuous, unstinted, vociferous and enthusiastic cooperation. We see their photographs as the evocative part of the book. We also thank several tutorial staff who joined in at times. We thank the technicians, especially 'Harry', who gave us voluntary help when our own manual dexterity proved to be inadequate in making materials. And we thank Christine for all the extra work she did in the typing and clerical work.

We thank the head teachers of the schools in which some of the work was carried out, in particular George Murray, Headmaster of Alderbury School, for his cooperation in the Stonehenge project, and Kenneth Haslam, then Headmaster of Highfield School, Chorley, and now Headmaster of Brockworth County Primary School, Gloucestershire, who tolerated and even encouraged the turmoil produced by the building of the Wendy House. Also we thank Mr Kenneth Hill, now Headmaster of Walney South Junior School, Barrow-in-Furness, in whose school at Crawshawbooth the photographs for Chapter Two were taken.

To Donald Haslam (the editor) and Pergamon Press (the publishers) of the journal *Primary Mathematics*, we are indebted for permission to re-use material that members of the team had already published in that journal. We thank Routledge & Kegan Paul for permission to quote some of Piaget's own words and to reproduce the shapes on page 37.

The other person to whom I would have liked to be able to express my gratitude is the late Nathan Isaacs, who gave me great encouragement and valuable advice in the early stages of this work. His book, *The Growth of Understanding in the Young Child*,[1] helped me considerably in making Chapter One simple and brief. Apart from this book, no books or articles have been used except the original translations of the books written by Piaget and his co-authors. To him, of course, the most gratitude of all is offered.

Members of the team who contributed substantially to the book are: Mr Norman Ellis, Mrs Audrey Green, Mr Frederick Jones, Mr Harvey Long, Mrs Betty Pennington, Mr Anthony Todd, Mr Deryck Weston, Mr John Woodcock, Mr Kenneth Worrall.

Mary Sime

24 March 1972

Principal Lecturer in Education,
Chorley College of Education,
Chorley, Lancashire.

[1] Published by Ward Lock Educational Company Ltd.

Section A:
The Child and his Environment

Derek. First attempt. Anxiety, failure.

INTRODUCTION

Who can reveal to us how a child learns and how he matures intellectually?

In a highly scientific and clinically valid way Professor Jean Piaget can do so. And only children themselves can demonstrate his findings to us. In a spontaneous and vivid manner, they can give us such demonstrations even without clinical facilities.

Nathan Isaacs, in a valuable condensed summary[1] of some of Piaget's works, says: 'The child, at about four years old enriches, works over, organises and re-organises his model of the world . . . through exploring and experimenting. The different kinds of objects and happenings which he can recognise, pre-adjust to, remember and imagine constantly increase.'

With this quotation in mind, we let Derek introduce this book with his reactions on first seeing a real violin at the age of three years and nine months.

Derek was a television addict at that age, so he recognized a violin as something to go under his chin: his anxious facial expression remained unbroken as he struggled, for some moments, before adjusting to a better idea.

As a double bass this new 'toy' certainly emitted sounds and so his anxiety gave way to ephemeral interest.

Pure delight showed on his face from the moment that he converted his toy into a guitar. His joy was complete and lasting. He had adapted it to himself and himself to the violin.

'The child is architect of his own growth', says Nathan Isaacs, in the same short book. Every such experience as this one of Derek's with the violin adds one further point of strength to the developing architecture. It becomes part of his internalized model of his world.

Derek. Second idea. Some success and anxiety eliminated.

Derek. Complete contentment.

[1] Quotations from Nathan Isaacs, *The Growth of Understanding in the Young Child*; Ward Lock Educational Company Ltd.

CHAPTER ONE
Piaget's basic theories

Piaget's work has shown us that a great deal of what we accepted from children in the past as evidence of true learning, or perhaps as evidence of mathematical or scientific ability, was, in fact, only a flimsy edifice on an insecure foundation.

Many children learned the mechanical tricks, especially of mathematical processes, without understanding the logical basis or the logical processes involved. What is, perhaps, more important is that the psychological feeling of insecurity that these children developed, because of this lack of understanding, resulted in their having no appreciation of the beauty of the rhythm and symmetry of mathematics, nor appreciation of the fascination of science. Nor did they get any pleasure from solving the mathematical and logical and scientific problems that came their way.

PERIODS OF INTELLECTUAL GROWTH[1]

An understanding of the developmental psychology of children, as revealed by Piaget, starts in the following way. He sees the intellectual growth of a young person as developing through a series of periods. The sequence of these periods is important, but the ages at which different children reach any period can vary considerably, so that the figures given below must be read as approximate.

Period 1 The sensory-motor period

This is the period, generally until about two years old, during which the baby is gaining experience through his senses and absorbing it into himself as patterns of behaviour. Piaget uses

[1] Jean Piaget & Bärbel Inhelder, *The Psychology of the Child*.

the word 'assimilation' for the simple, straightforward absorbing of such experience and 'accommodation' for the adaptation that goes on when the 'schema' built up by previous experience has to be adapted to new, and perhaps unexpected, experience.

This absorption of sensory-motor experience and enrichment of schemata goes on all our lives, throughout all the periods that have still to be listed below. It is this interaction between the human being and his environment (i.e. the actions of the person influencing his environment with the environment, in turn, causing an intellectual development in the person) that is a basic theme of all Piaget's work.

During the sensory-motor period the child begins to use language. This is made possible as a result of his 'generalizing' certain repeated experiences, creating a thought out of the common property in them and being able to symbolize this thought by a word. From now onwards he can sometimes represent the experience by the thought or a word, but only if the experience is of a well-worn action (e.g. 'play', 'run') or object (e.g. 'Teddy bear').

Period 2 The preconceptual period

This period, in most children, lasts until about the age of four. During this period the child's intellectual growth lies in the building up of ideas or notions (i.e. 'pre-concepts') that in the next period will become 'concepts' founded upon an appreciation of the common properties in classes of things and of actions. During this preconceptual period, however, the notions are very shaky and ephemeral because the child is still not clear as to whether, for example, the snail he sees in his garden is the same snail as the one that he sees later, a mile away, or whether the sun he sees today is the same sun that he saw yesterday. He is not sure that the milk poured from a bottle into his cup remains absolutely and exactly the same milk. Some of these insecurities last well into the next period. Piaget would say that, intellectually, the child has not attained conservation of matter.

Period 3 The intuitive period

This period lasts, in most children, throughout infants' school life and very often throughout the first year in the junior school. It is the period during which many of the basic concepts are being formed. If a child's education is badly handled at this time the concepts can be prevented from forming healthily, or a distorted alternative substitute concept can form. A concept, like a schema before it, becomes an integral and dynamic part of a child's self. It is not just a notion or an idea but a distillation from

13

many notions that becomes part of the whole organism and that can trigger off lines of mental activity in him. It is because of the importance of concept formation for an understanding of the theories of Piaget, and particularly for adapting his theories to the learning of mathematics, that no more will be said about it at this point. Instead it is dealt with fully below, together with photographic illustrations of children's stages of forming some concepts.

Period 4 The concrete operational period

This period generally lasts throughout the junior school and across the first year or two of secondary school life. The key point about this period is that the child has generally formed concepts of very simple classification, of seriation, of number, of length, of area, etc., and he is forming concepts of weight and, later, of volume. These are all concepts that have been abstracted from material things, and they enable him to take an interest in problems that involve further material things (or clear memories of them). He can solve such problems as long as the material things are available to help support each process in his thoughts at each stage in the problem. By thus experimenting with materials he watches for possible answers to his problem, gets practice in discussing results with his peers and with his parents and his teachers, probes for explanations, perhaps records results (in words or graphically or diagramatically) on paper as well as mentally. He is, however, still unable to hypothesize a solution and set out, systematically, to prove or disprove it.

Period 5 The period of formal thinking

This final period, which could be divided into two subperiods, develops during adolescence in most people, although in some of us it is never reached. Very simply, it is the period in which most of us become able to reason abstractly — to hypothesize and work from the abstract to the particular, instead of the other way round, or even to work from the abstract to the abstract. During this period we form and use concepts from abstractions, such as concepts of proportion (i.e. of a relationship between relationships), of law, of justice, of infinity, and so forth.

These new operations and concepts are called 'formal' ones because they take on a form (linked also with the word 'formula') that results from thinking about abstractions, as contrasted to abstracting generalizations from concrete evidence. The whole experience is just as 'real' as the earlier concrete experiences were, but it is purely intellectual. Often it is the action of concepts working upon other concepts.

14

For example, the interaction of the concept of 'justice' (a purely abstract notion) upon the concept of 'expediency' (another abstract notion) can produce the concept of 'law' (also abstract) and can lead a teenager to hypothesize about the unlikely and even about the impossible.

Piaget claims that the form of such adolescent and adult reasoning (i.e. of 'formal reasoning') takes on patterns of mental activity similar to the mathematical processes in 'groups' and 'lattices'. This has been illustrated as simply as possible in the chapter on the child's understanding, at different stages, of equilibrium in the balance.[2]

Similarly, other chapters will, one at a time, report on how Piaget examined the development of many of the concepts and patterns of thinking that enable a child to grow up into a reasoning human being: in all cases, Piaget's experiments have been repeated with English children so that photographic illustration can help clarify the written word.

Piaget's investigations follow developmental psychology right through adolescence, showing us the whole magnificence of the intellectual processes in which the primary school child is at the early stages. They can be mentioned only briefly here but this glance forward at them re-emphasizes the importance of the early stages as foundation stages. In these early stages, active, enjoyable and significant experiences lay firm foundations for later firm intellectual growth.

PIAGET'S METHODS OF TESTING

Piaget was by no means the first psychologist or philosopher to attempt to convince us of the child-centredness of learning. Dewey, Rousseau, Comenius, Froebel and even Aristotle and Plato preceded him in that. But Piaget is the first to give us quite such a wealth of detail about specific children's ideas of the world around them. He himself is perhaps the first outstanding psychologist to report these ideas as each being of value in itself rather then reporting them by reducing them to statistics.[3] Also he has shown us how to test children's thinking for qualitative rather than quantitative results. He uses these ideas as illustrations of the routes that intellectual development takes in the growth of the young child and of the adolescent.

Children's convictions

In some of his earliest works such as *The Child's Conception of The World*, he used the technique of listening to the questions that children asked either of adults or of other children: he then asked different children those same questions. By so doing, he

---

[2] See Chapter Ten. Also see Chapter Twelve for 'lattices'. Piagetian references *The Growth of Logical Thinking*, Chapters Eleven and Thirteen.

[3] The only book in which Piaget makes much use of statistics is *The Early Growth of Logic in the Child*.

had taken care that the subject-matter really interested children and was not extraneous to their normal thinking.

The answers he received lead us to understand that, in the course of being socialized as he grows up, a child's convictions are of three sorts:

1 Those swallowed whole from adults either through indoctrination or from being overheard.
2 Those influenced, but not dictated, by adults.
3 Convictions that are the original reaction of the child to his world. These can be either (*a*) liberated conviction or (*b*) spontaneous conviction.
(*a*) Liberated conviction is shown when a child speaks his thought out loud as he reasons. It reveals to us his natural trend of thinking.
(*b*) Spontaneous conviction is the result of *previous* original reflection. By his statements the child shows that he is sure that he knows an answer.

In the liberated conviction category[4] come such convictions as that the sun pushes the clouds along, that the clouds make the wind, that many inanimate things are alive, that names are part of the objects they define or that fire can feel anger and malice. Such convictions, solidly held by many children, resist suggestion or attempted correction by adults. Their notions about 'thought' are particularly interesting. Toddlers generally do not know what thinking means: young infants may believe that we think with our mouths, and slightly older ones, while realizing that we think in our heads, consider that thought is something as concrete as a voice inside the head. Children know that they know things but have no idea as to the origin of their knowledge. This is why they can so often easily be convinced that an imposed idea was their own. Why do we need to know that they think this way? Surely, as a 'caveat', to warn us that their statements, which, in some cases, may seem to us to be absolute lies, can have resulted from thinking of this sort. Even their solutions to mathematical problems might be equally imaginative.

In all his earlier books Piaget used verbal methods of probing children's thoughts. He has been severely criticized for the inexactness of the method and for too easily jumping to conclusions. In spite of this criticism, many of his earlier books still sell well, to the extent that some are now produced in paperback editions.

Concept formation[5]

All his later works, the ones to which most emphasis is given in this book, are based on the use of a method of investigation that

[4] Jean Piaget, *The Child's Conception of Physical Causality*, Chapter 2; Routledge & Kegan Paul.
[5] Jean Piaget, *The Child's Conception of Number, et alia.*

is far more scientifically valid, though equally simple and personal. The thoughts of each child who is tested are again examined qualitatively rather than quantitatively. In every case very simple, yet highly ingenious, apparatus is put before the child and he is asked to do simple actions and to express his thoughts in words. The skill of the testing comes in the supplementary questioning that follows as a result of each of the child's responses, for the purpose of the testing is to reveal what the child really thinks and to guard against inadvertently implying possible answers or in any way suggesting them to him. No answer is really valid unless the child is genuinely interested in what he is doing or saying, and no right answer is valid unless it is given for the right reasons.

A few of the best known of the very simple Piagetian tests about a child's understanding of such abstractions as number, length, area, sequence are illustrated by the following examples. The tests were carried out in what was known as the 'puzzle corner' of a children's club — a corner to which children gravitated when they tired of table-tennis, clay modelling, woodwork, music-making and other such recreations. The materials, simple as they are, were sufficiently enticing to draw children temporarily from the other pleasures. They need not be described as they can be seen clearly in the photographs that follow.

Child's conception of number[6]
STAGE I: Martin was quite unable to see the 1:1 correspondence between seven eggs and seven egg-cups although he enjoyed

Martin. Concept of number. Stage I.

[6] Jean Piaget & A. Szeminska, *The Child's Conception of Number*, Chapters 3 and 4.

Jane. Concept of number. Stage II.

Susan. Concept of number. Stage III.

18

playing at transferring the eggs from the carton to the cups. When faced with eight eggs instead of seven he was bewildered about what to do with the last one.

STAGE II: Jane, when faced with two rows of discs, was able to 'count' the seven discs in each row. While the rows were identically spaced, she agreed that there were the same number of discs in each. As soon as the visual pattern of 1:1 correspondence was disturbed she insisted, 'There are more in the bottom row now they are all squashed up.'

STAGE III: Susan does not need 1:1 correspondence. She can go and fetch enough cartons of milk for all at the table to have one each.

Concept of area[7]

The children were given two green, foam-rubber 'fields', which they agreed were identical in size (and Penelope made sure that the grass was the same length on each). All the children shown agreed that the cows each had the same amount of grass to eat and of field to wander over. Identical houses were added simultaneously, one by one, and each time the question was repeated, 'Have the cows still the same amount of grass left for each?'

STAGES I AND II: Jane was bored by being delayed by such questioning and only waited to get a chance to play freely with the toy. Penelope, in contrast, was interested and seemed to be getting a vague idea of what 'area' was all about. So long as the houses were placed in corresponding positions on each field

Jane and Penelope. Concept of area. Stages I and II.

[7] Jean Piaget, Bärbel Inhelder & A. Szeminska, *The Child's Conception of Geometry*, Chapter 1.

Jacqueline and Janet. Concept of area.
Stages I and II.

Jacqueline and Janet. Concept of area.
Stages I and II.

Michael. Concept of area. Stage III.

she agreed that the same amount of grassland remained for each cow but as soon as the similarity of visual pattern was broken, by clustering the houses more on one field than on the other, she became very puzzled and generally decided that one or other of the fields had more land than the other left for grazing. ALSO AT STAGES I AND II: Jacqueline and Janet both considered that scattered houses took up more of the field than did closely built ones. Janet was adamant about it while there were only two houses on each field but Jacqueline was not shaken until the number was rather greater than that. 'However,' she explained, 'you could make it the same if you put them like this', and proceeded to move the scattered ones into the same pattern as those on the first field.

STAGE III: Michael was just at Stage III. He asked to be left alone for a time to work it all out. Then he came up with the answer: 'It's always the same left on each field if the number of houses is the same — wherever you put them.'

Concept of serial ordering[8]

Children were faced with the problem of hanging garments (from an excess supply) on a second line (a) in similar order and (b) in reverse order, to that on a specimen line.

[8] Jean Piaget & Bärbel Inhelder, *The Child's Conception of Space*, Chapter 3.

STAGE I: Catherine, at first, seemed to understand the question but soon got carried away by her enthusiasm and hung every available garment on the line. She was completely uninterested in matching sequence. Catherine needed a helper beside her to dispense Scotch tape and she soon began to demand that he pass her the garments; she was adamant, each time, about which one she needed next and seemed to be choosing aesthetically.

STAGE II: Susan Jane managed quite well to hang the parallel line with garments in similar order to those on the top line, obviously carrying out the task by 1:1 correspondence. When it came to reverse ordering she was helped in putting on the first trousers on the left end of the line. Then she continued, with some struggling and supporting her efforts with a running commentary aloud, and was accurate until she reached the middle garment on the line. After this her carefully reasoned actions gave way to the comfortable ease of following a visible 1:1 correspondence, so she completed the line in direct, instead of reverse, order. Then she telephoned at once to say, 'The washing is nearly dry.'

A child at Stage III would be able to envisage the result immediately on facing the problem.

Catherine. Concept of serial ordering. Stage I.

Susan Jane. Concept of serial ordering. Stage II.

Ian. Concept of linear and circular order.
Stage II.

Concept of linear and circular order[9]

STAGE II: Ian was faced with a Piagetian problem very similar to that of the reversal on the linen line. He was shown a string of beads, threaded on a circular wire, and was asked to thread other beads in similar order on a straight wire. At his first attempt he 'got lost' after threading a few beads, so he started again. He is a cautious, thoughtful little boy. At the second attempt he took care to slide along, on the circular wire, the bead that he was matching on the straight wire, thus enabling himself to solve the problem by 1:1 correspondence. Now that he had eliminated the need to remember (i.e. to build on hindsight), or to see ahead in the solution, he was able to complete the threading accurately. A child at Stage I would be more confused than Ian, while a child at Stage III would envisage clearly what to do without resorting so laboriously to 1:1 correspondence.

[9] Jean Piaget & Bärbel Inhelder, *The Child's Conception of Space*, Chapter 3.

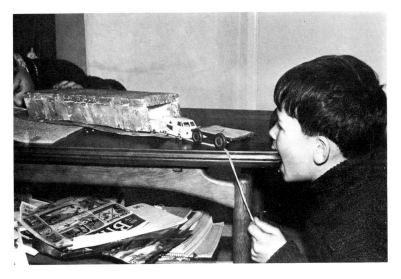

Michael. Concept of movement in sequence.
Stage III.

Concept of movement in sequence[10]

Michael was shown a toy tunnel and a train of three carriages. When he had examined them, the carriages were hidden inside the tunnel while he watched: he was placed at the side of the tunnel and was asked: (*a*) in which sequence they would come out at A; (*b*) in which sequence they would come out at B. He answered correctly. Again he watched them being hidden in the tunnel and the orientation of the tunnel was changed (with the train inside it) through two right angles. The questions were repeated and were answered correctly. On the third test, Michael's position was changed while the train was hidden. On the fourth test the tunnel was reorientated and Michael's position was changed. On all tests he answered correctly. Afterwards he was puzzled enough to want to examine why it all happened that way.

This example of results on what might seem a difficult test is quoted to show how young a child may start forming a concept if he gains early and valuable experience. As Michael said, he had played with trains at home.

Concept of occupied and unoccupied space[11]

Robert was asked whether the space between the Red Indians remained the same when a polythene 'brick wall' was placed between them. Like most children of his age, he was convinced that the space was now less. This sort of response opened up a whole line of study for Piaget who points out that, to a child, 'space' is only space so long as it is unoccupied: he has no concept of occupied space. This is to some extent another

[10] Jean Piaget, *The Child's Conception of Movement and Speed*, Chapter 1.
[11] Jean Piaget, Bärbel Inhelder & A. Szeminska, *The Child's Conception of Geometry*, Chapter 3.

Robert. Concept of occupied and
unoccupied space. Stage II.

example of the impact upon the senses overruling one's thinking.
This seems less incredible when we force ourselves to realize that
most of us, even as adults, have at some time made such a
remark as: 'Isn't the room bigger now that the piano is taken out?'

Conclusion

The foregoing examples all show children at one of the three
main stages of forming concepts about abstract properties that
are related to, as contrasted to being inherent in, the materials
they are handling. It is no longer the properties of eggs or of egg-
cups that we are asking Martin about, but the abstract property
of 'sevenness' that is common to the seven eggs and seven cups.
It is about the abstract property of equal area that we were
testing Michael's reasoning, not the properties of cows or of
fields.

The youngest of the children had little or no idea of what numbers meant. He knew the difference between 'an egg' and 'a lot
of eggs', but, to him, number, as adults would understand it, was
blurred. Yet he could be trained to the parrot-like repetition of
reciting numbers.

In contrast, Jane had just started on the path of forming a notion
of the 'sevenness' in each line of counters. She was beginning
to realize that 'seven' could be applied to collections of widely
differing objects. But 'sevenness' was not yet a notion that she

24

could hold steady in her thoughts as something indestructible. She relied more on her sense of sight than on this beginning of a notion and accepted blandly that the number of counters could increase or decrease as the visual pattern was changed. 'Seven' meant nothing stable to her. Piaget would say that she had not yet completely 'abstracted' the property of 'seven' from the counters, but that she was a stage nearer to doing so than was Martin.

Susan was at a still more mature stage. For her, the number 'six' conserved its own character whether it was represented by children or by milk cartons, whether by scattered objects or by a similar number of objects in neat array. The actual number, as well as the objects, had an immediate impact on her.

Susan was also convinced that the property of 'six' could not be destroyed, whatever happened to the milk cartons. If two were removed the reverse action of bringing in two more would restore the number to six again. She was, therefore, a stage ahead of Jane in her development of a notion of the meaning of a number.

This does not necessarily mean that Susan had a secure concept of number, although a concept was now growing rapidly. She just had a clear notion of the 'sixness' of 'six' and, incidentally, of the 'sevenness' of 'seven' and of the values of many other small numbers. Constant practice with many numbers will gradually produce in her a dynamic sense of appreciation of the whole range of numbers from nought to infinity, of their indestructibility, of their relationships to each other, of their abstractness from the things that are used to represent them. Ultimately, she will not need 'things to represent them': numbers will be as 'real' in her thoughts as are material things. In other words, she will have developed a concept of number. The dynamism of this concept is one of its important features. It is now an integral part of her whole organism and it can, if roused, trigger off intellectual activities just as surely as her limbs can trigger off physical activities. And, just as her limbs can be used as tools in helping to achieve physical goals, so can this concept of number, or any other concept, come into action as a tool to help reach an intellectual goal. All these earliest concepts emerge as abstractions from active physical and mental response to material things. As has been said earlier, later concepts result from active mental response to abstract ideas. But all concepts are alike in that they have become dynamic parts of the human being who has nurtured them in himself through his interaction with his environment.

It is this line of thought that is reported on and illustrated in the chapters that follow.

CHAPTER TWO

A study of children's ideas about horizontality[1]

Piaget suggests[2] that the most natural spatial frame of reference to the child is probably that provided by the world around him in the shape of the vertical and horizontal axes of natural objects. He goes on to test children's appreciation of these axes by questioning the children about the levels of liquids in masked bottles that are tilted at various angles: through these tests he has revealed to us that many children of infant-school age have little idea about the phenomenon of the surfaces of liquids finding their own level.

A young teacher noticed a practical example of this when the infants, who had previously enjoyed milk from glass bottles, were suddenly confronted instead with opaque plastic milk cartons. Many of the children became thwarted and confused through being unable to locate the position of the milk once their cartons were half empty. Many, in fact, began to cease to take morning milk and most of the rest left considerable quantities of milk undrunk in the cartons.

Application of the Piagetian tests and comparison of the results with the children's antics as they tried to locate milk in the cartons revealed an intriguing correlation, of which the following four examples are typical. They show clearly the stages that Piaget would lead us to expect.

In each case the child was shown a set of glass bottles after he had finished drinking his milk from the carton. He was also shown empty drawn shapes of the bottles and he was only tested further if he could match the bottles to the drawn shapes.

When he had achieved the matching he was helped to pour some milk into one of the bottles and was asked to point out the line of the surface of the milk.

[1] This chapter was prepared by Audrey Green and Mary Sime.
[2] Jean Piaget & Bärbel Inhelder, *The Child's Conception of Space*, Chapter 13.

The bottle was then wrapped in a small, thin cloth (so as not to mask its shape) and was tilted as shown on the drawings. The child was asked to point out, on the masked bottle, where he thought the milk was and where its surface was. He was allowed to see how correct he had been. The bottle was then masked again and he was asked to mark on the remasked bottle and then to transfer to the drawn bottle the position of the milk in the masked bottle. The test was repeated for each bottle in turn. In almost every case the children drew in the positioning that they had estimated before seeing the bottle unmasked. So far the investigation is a repetition of the one devised by Piaget and recorded in *The Child's Conception of Space*.

The illustrations overleaf show photographs of children attempting to drink their milk, and also show photostats of their drawings of estimated positions of the milk in the masked bottles.

STAGE I: Caroline, who tipped the carton until the milk ran down her chin, while her straw remained in the air-pocket above the milk, drew vague blobs to show the position of where she expected the milk to be in each masked bottle. Her whole idea of where the milk might be was guesswork, not only as shown in her drawings, but also as she attempted to point out its whereabouts on the actual masked bottle.

In other words, Caroline had not even noticed the positioning of the milk in the bottle, nor had she any idea where it would be in the carton.

STAGE IIa: Philip expected the milk to stay approximately parallel to the bottom of the bottle at whatever angle the bottle was tilted. He also expected it to stay at the bottom of the bottle even when the bottle was inverted. A temporary unveiling did not convince him to the contrary. In the plastic carton he tried, as the photograph shows, to find it in an approximately similar position.

STAGE IIb: Beverley had realized that the milk does not stay near the bottom of the bottle, though she was unsure of where it does stay. Through constant experiment, shown in the photograph, for example by her bending of the straw, she was almost subconsciously gaining information that will later build up in her into a generalization and later still into an understanding and finally into a concept of the laws of horizontality.

STAGE III: Mark could find his milk in the carton with confidence. He could also draw in its position by prediction and after seeing it. But, especially before the bottle was unmasked, he was a little unsure of the shape of the surface.

27

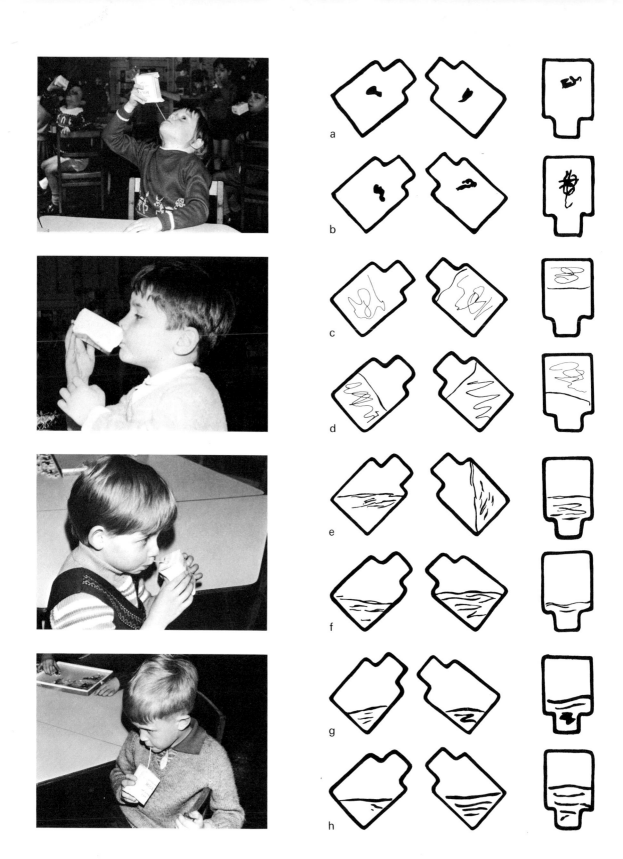

Concluding statement

The conclusion is best represented by a question, since none of the children tested was at a stage of certainty (Stage IIIb). Can we afford plastic milk cartons instead of glass bottles in the infants' school? Or, instead, will constant experimenting in their search for milk prove of educational rather than nutritional value, helping the children to develop a concept of horizontality even if they leave much of the milk undrunk?

Addendum

Further observation, since this chapter was written, has shown us that the children who continue to drink milk do, in fact, learn from experience where to find the milk. It would be interesting to retest such children with the Piagetian tests, to see whether such learning can be applied to the masked bottles or whether it has only reached the intuitive stage.

From top to bottom:

Caroline. Stage I.
  a Caroline's advance estimate.
  b Caroline's drawing after seeing the milk.
Philip. Stage IIa.
  c Philip's advance estimate.
  d Philip's drawing after seeing the milk.
Beverley. Stage IIb.
  e Beverley's advance estimate.
  f Beverley's estimate after seeing the milk.
Mark. Stage III.
  g Mark's advance estimate.
  h Mark's estimate after seeing the milk.

29

CHAPTER THREE

Children's pre-mathematical ideas about perspective[1]

Piaget, in testing young children in such a way as to penetrate their real, deep understanding of, and misconceptions about, the spatial layout of the objects that they see around them,[2] has reached results that give us a warning. It is that, in most infant and junior children, there is insufficient pre-mathematical foundation for them to understand, as contrasted to achieving mechanically, many of the tasks that adults set them involving reproduction of maps and charts, map-drawing (e.g. in history or geography studies) and any arithmetical or even literary studies that pose problems on moving objects or on changes of positions.

Students training to be teachers find it interesting and instructive to repeat some of Piaget's tests. Some young teachers themselves find it very surprising that mathematical concepts are at the basis of subjects as apparently 'arts'-focused as history, geography, literature and even art itself. Parents may equally well find examples of this difficulty as they travel around with their children. Yet, the very travel helps the children to overcome it.

The tests described below are re-enactments of those carried out by Piaget. Children from the ages of four to twelve were tested. The model of three mountains, unequal in height and differently coloured, was sufficiently pleasing aesthetically to encourage the younger ones to consider it as a toy. Templates of the side-on view of each mountain were prepared, and correspondingly coloured, in advance of the testing and also eight pictures of the views as seen from the sides and corners of the model were painted.

The purpose of the testing was to try to discover to what extent each child could appreciate that people seeing the model from a

---

[1] Chapter prepared by Mary Sime and John Woodcock.
[2] Jean Piaget & Bärbel Inhelder, *The Child's Conception of Space*, Chapter 8.

different position from his own would perceive a view of the mountains that was different from the one he was seeing. The young teachers also made rough estimates as to what extent variation of the stages of ability seemed to run parallel with those of chronological age, and tried to investigate whether other influences, such as home environment, favourite toys, or week-end jaunts to mountainous areas, were equally influential to, or even more influential than, age.

Insufficient numbers of children were tested (about thirty) to come to any generalized conclusions, but the most interesting of the individual results are published below.

Each child who volunteered to 'come and play' was invited to sit at any side of the model that he chose and to get his chin down to the ground-level of the model. At first the adult who was testing him sat opposite him and did the same. The child was then asked to do the following tasks: in the case of young children an element of play was brought into the questioning, such as 'cowboys and Indians'.

Test 1
To lay the templates over one another so that he built up a picture of his own view of the mountains.

Test 2
To recognize, from a choice of the eight pictures, which one was the view from his own position.

If he could not do either of these tasks correctly it was clear that his perceptual abilities were such that the tests were meaningless to him and, although he was allowed to play with the model for a time, he was tested no further.

If he could do either of the above tasks satisfactorily he was then asked:

Test 3
To build, with the templates, the view as seen by the tester sitting opposite him.

Test 4
To select from the eight pictures the view that the tester was seeing.

Several of the children who had achieved correct results for Tests 1 and 2 repeated exactly the same results for solutions to Tests 3 and 4. These children did not even consider that there was a possibility of a different view from their own. Others, at a very slightly more advanced stage of mental development, chose pictures completely by guesswork for Test 4 (and also for Tests 6 and 8 (below)), suggesting that they did, at least, suppose that the other view was different from their own.

31

Tests 5, 6, 7 and 8

These were similar to Tests 3 and 4 except that the tester asked the questions from the child's right and then from his left. Only a few children who answered all these questions correctly were asked to estimate the views from the corners of the board.

Results

Very marked stages could be seen in the development of children's realizations of their own and of other people's points of view. The first was a stage (Stage I) at which children could not even consider any of the questions. Then came the 'egocentric' stage (Stage IIa) at which children could describe the view they saw but did not even realize that another point of view existed. At Stage IIb they became vaguely aware that there was a chance of other views but they were quite unable to imagine them. At Stage IIIa a child began to be able to construct views other than his own but was extremely insecure in doing so; perhaps he would get an opposite view correct and fail on the side ones, or be correct when using templates and incorrect at sorting pictures, or vice versa. By Stage IIIb, he could do most of the tests correctly and others like them. Only one child was given the hardest test of all — that of drawing freehand an opposite viewpoint with no help from templates and/or pictures.

Examples of the children at particular stages are reproduced on the following pages, together with the pictures that they built from the templates. As often as possible photographs have been chosen which show, by the children's glances, where the tester is standing.

STAGE I: Scott had no idea what the questions were about. He did, however, see great fun in scampering over the mountains with rapid 'walking-finger' movements in a mock attack on the tester. A further example of a response typical of nursery school children entertained us when none of the children could pay any attention to the questions, but they found various games they could play with the model, including a final game of flicking the scree at one another and taking cover behind mountains.

STAGE IIa: Andrew was just able to construct his own view (which, in the picture, he has turned round to show the tester) but he reconstructed the same picture whichever view he was asked for.

STAGE IIb: Robert was very puzzled as to whether or not there could be another view. He considered this for a long time and made several attempts, but eventually decided that every view he was asked for was the same as his own.

Scott, Stage I, plays with the model.

Andrew, Stage IIa, shows his own view as
the view from opposite to him.

Robert, Stage IIb, is puzzled about a
possible different view.

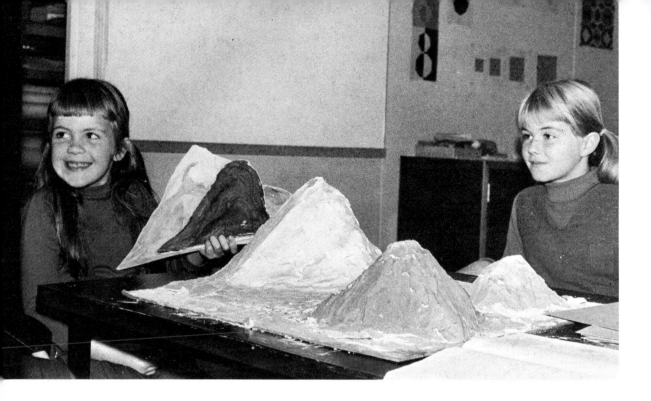

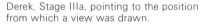

Tricia, Stage IIb–IIIa, showing the view from her right.

Derek, Stage IIIa, pointing to the position from which a view was drawn.

AN OVERLAP OF STAGES IIb AND IIIa: Tricia was correct about her own view and was occasionally correct about left and right views, but she was defeated by reverse-order ones and constructed them as from her own position. She fluctuated at different times between the two stages. In comparison with other children of her age she was advanced. The young teachers attributed this to the facts that, since her babyhood, her parents have been in overseas service and until very recently she has been taken on frequent flights and on other journeys in hilly and mountainous country. Now she goes on week-end photographing expeditions with her father in the Lake District. She is constantly discussing views.

STAGE IIIa (but very borderline): Derek was quite sure that other views were different from his own and he was frequently right on any one of the Tests 1–8 so far quoted. He often hesitated for a long time before deciding on an answer and, when he felt sure of a view, he jumped about in delight clutching the picture or the built-up templates. He was not given other tests to corroborate his placings in IIIa. He was very young indeed to be at such a stage and he showed the childlike tendency of frequently breaking off from the matter in hand to play with the toy. His advanced ability seemed, possibly, to be due to constant playing of 'I spy' with his parents and sisters, and to a lavish supply of toys that have mathematical values.

34

STAGE III*a*: Alison Catherine was generally right in her answers, but tended to make some mistakes when the views of small mountains were obliterated by larger ones. She is Tricia's sister and often goes on the photographing expeditions already described. The photograph depicts her showing the view from her own left.

Alison Catherine, Stage III*a*, showing a view as seen from a corner.

STAGE III*b*: Alison Jacqueline, when given the tests so far described, was fully able to co-ordinate all perspectives. When given the further, much more difficult, test of being asked to draw a freehand picture, as if from a corner position (not near to her own) and without any help from templates or from pictures, she was correct in her positioning of the various heights but made no allowance for the different widths of the mountains.

Alison Jacqueline, Stage III*b*, drawing a view from a distant corner.

Sandra and Angela, both in fourth-year junior school, were tested in each other's presence. In some tests it was carefully arranged that no element of competition could creep in and in other comparable tests the challenge was made into a competitive game. In the non-competitive tests Sandra made fewer mistakes than Angela, though both had very real difficulties in constructing views from their left and right. In the competitive games, however, Sandra, who is rather timid, lost her earlier vivacity and seemed unable to make up her mind about answers. Angela's answers were of the same standard as in the non-competitive testing.

35

Concluding statement

From these examples we can see that it is possible that all factors such as age, general development, environment, habits about games and competition or lack of it, appear to influence a child's understanding of spatial layout. We can all, as parents or teachers, set out to influence most of these factors and to enrich a child's chances of building a safe concept of co-ordinating perspectives. We can also be very cautious about not confusing any child's development by giving him tasks that could confuse the growth of this concept, particularly by refraining from giving him maps (which are abstract symbols) before we know he can imagine the views they represent from other than his own point of view.

CHAPTER FOUR
Topology – or 'india rubber geometry'

A small group of young teachers, who were studying Piaget's *The Child's Conception of Space*,[1] specifically Chapter 2, were absorbed in observing children's reactions to drawing geometrical shapes.[2] Piaget claims that children mature to an appreciation of Euclidean properties (straight or curved lines, angles, equalities, etc.), through stages of appreciating only the topological features of closed or open shapes, of inclusion, of exclusion, of crossing and so forth; i.e. of Euclidean figures withstanding the distortions of stretching in any directions. We set forth to search for illustrations of this theory and to ponder on how far the sophisticated home and school backgrounds of children today may hasten the speed of passing through these stages.

We illustrate here a few typical examples, from among many, of the work of children, each of whom was tested twice (a year apart) on copying the shapes.
All photographs were taken at the first of these two testings.
As with all Piagetian testing, results showed clearly that each child's stage of development was far more significant than was his chronological age.
STAGE 0 TO I*a*: Rosanne, the daughter of an art tutor, progressed from Stage 0 (pure scribble) to Stage I*a* (in which her scribble was slightly influenced in shape by what she saw). This is strikingly parallel with what Piaget describes for Swiss children of the same age. (Photograph taken at age 3:3 years.)
STAGE I TO II: Derek, who was well into Stage I at 2:0 years, attempted to reproduce most topological properties, such as enclosure or crossing. At 3:0 years, he had learned to reproduce strange shapes. Yet he was entering Piaget's Stage II by trying

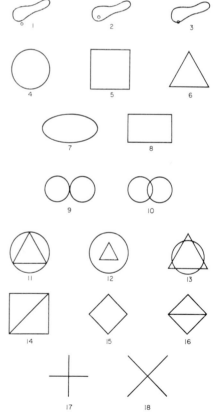

The topological shapes that Piaget asked the children to draw.

[1] Routledge & Kegan Paul.
[2] Diagram of the shapes that Piaget used, reproduced from *The Child's Conception of Space* with the permission of Routledge & Kegan Paul.

Rosanne, Stage 0, at 3:3 years. Her
drawing is pure scribble.

Rosanne's drawing at 4:3 years. Stage I.

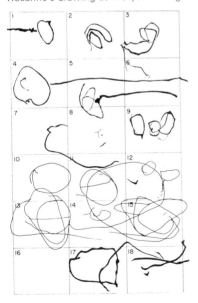

Derek. Stage I

to distinguish: (*a*) straight from curved lines, and (*b*) angular shapes, as well as topological properties. His advanced ability could well be partly due to a background rich in scribbling materials, to toys and books, and to the loving attention of two bright elder sisters. A photostat of some of his work is shown.

STAGE II*a* TO II*b*: Judith, attending a nursery school in which she was encouraged to play with shapes and to draw, was entering Stage II at 4:0 years: she was reasonably secure in topological shapes, except complicated ones such as shape 13, and was becoming interested in Euclidean properties, though most rectilinear shapes (shape 6) still had one curved side. At 5:0 years straight lines were firmly distinguished from curved ones, though shape 13 still defeated her.

Shape 17

Derek's drawing at 2:0 years. Stage I.

Derek's drawing at 3:0 years. Stage II.

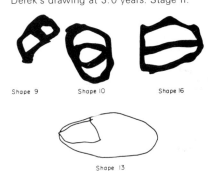

Shape 9   Shape 10   Shape 16

Shape 13

Judith. Stage IIa.

Judith's drawing at 4:0 years. Stage IIa.

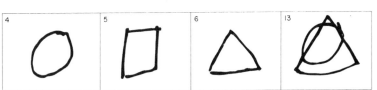

Judith's drawing at 5:0 years. Stage IIb.

Andrew. Stage IIa.

a Andrew's drawing at 5:7 years. Stage IIa.

b Andrew's drawing at 6:7 years. Stage IIb.

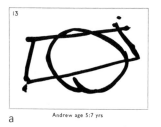

13

Andrew age 5:7 yrs

a

13

Andrew age 6:7 yrs

b

STAGE IIa TO IIb: Andrew spent the year in an infants' school gradually maturing through Stage II. His first results (5:7 years) can be seen in the photograph. At 6:7 years, he drew all the shapes correctly except shape 13, which we reproduce above. He puzzled us, as he was the only child at Stage II who seemed insecure about the topological properties of such shapes as 3 and 11, whereas even a year earlier, he had seen the Euclidean properties of many shapes.

STAGE III: Nicolas (6:5–7:5 years) drew all the shapes confidently and firmly at the first testing. For each figure he seemed to find a point of reference from which to move and abstract the shape: this even applied to shape 13 which can be seen clearly in the picture that we reproduce. A year later, he worked more quickly and very accurately.

Nicolas. Stage III.

41

Concluding statement

The conclusions we can draw from these examples are few and simple though quite vital. Topological properties of shapes in space are more meaningful to a very young child than are the Euclidean properties of such shapes. Yet, until recently in our schools, we have reserved topology for sixth-form grammar school learning. A young child is far more able to recognize and copy topological shapes than we have ever considered possible. He would not be able to copy these shapes if he were not appreciative of them. Such sense of appreciation would suggest that we would be justified in giving him far more scope than we have done in the past for investigating shapes, for playing with them and gradually appreciating and abstracting their properties, and for building and creative play with shapes. Further to this, by the age of about seven years most children are appreciating the Euclidean as well as topological properties of shapes. Hence, let us applaud the modern primary schools which introduce experience with shapes right from the reception class. But we must guard against complacency. More and more of our teachers need to have a thorough understanding of the mathematical foundations that can be laid in a child's mind by the teacher's judicious selection of what shapes to put temptingly before him, of when to encourage him in what he has chosen to build, and of how to recognize a potential geometrical development in a child's own original line of investigation. At home the child's parents can similarly enrich his environment. Over and above laying a foundation for the child's later intellectual development in mathematics, this wise provision of interestingly shaped playthings will prepare a child for later enjoyment of all the beauty in the symmetry and rhythm of mathematical thinking.

Section B:
Substructures for Logical Reasoning

INTRODUCTION

In this section, we illustrate a few of the basic ways in which children, more particularly young children, develop the ability to reason logically. Generally speaking, all of us use schemata and concepts, such as those that have been illustrated in Chapters One to Four, as tools in our reasoning: we might, therefore, consider that we cannot begin reasoning logically until at least we have formed our basic concepts.

Piaget and Inhelder, however, have led us to realize that very young infants, while they are still forming these basic concepts, are at the same time beginning to reason logically through fumbling attempts at classifying things that are alike and through looking for the relationships of things that can be put in logical series. Thus they gradually begin to see logical order in the world around them. At first 'pre-classification' is by trial and error. Gradually children begin to use memory and hindsight and then foresight in the process, so that they classify and seriate mentally. In his latest book Piaget says: 'The limit character of operations, as opposed to the simple "regulations" of earlier levels, means that, instead of corrections being made after the event, that is, once the action has been carried out physically, errors are pre-corrected in virtue of the interplay of direct and inverse operations, or, in other words, as we have just seen, as a result of the combinations of anticipations and retrospections themselves.'[1]

Piaget and Inhelder have devoted the whole book, *Early Growth of Logic in the Child*, to reporting on investigations as to how the skills of classifying and seriating develop in the years preceding the age of formal thought. In a way, it parallels their earlier work, *The Child's Conception of Space*, and it would be

[1] Jean Piaget, *Principles of Genetic Epistemology*, pp. 35–36.

well to read it before *The Growth of Logical Thinking from Childhood to Adolescence*, which is introduced here in Chapters Six and Seven, and then dealt with again in Section C.

The children illustrated in Chapter Six are still, predominantly, classifying. They are classifying 'floaters' and 'sinkers'. But, beyond this, they are working out *why* objects float and sink. To begin with, they hazard guesses, give them as reasons and do not see that they are contradicting their own statements. We cannot be logical if we contradict ourselves. Piaget and Inhelder examine how we grow through the process of eliminating these contradictions. When we observe interrelated movements or happenings, at what age do we begin to notice that one might imply that the other is inevitable? And then, how soon can we set out logically to ascertain whether that implication was true? With the help of a toy billiard-table, this is dealt with in Chapter Seven.

These fine lines of logical thinking have been gathered together in one section because quite a considerable part of their development takes place before and during the stage of concrete reasoning, although the final stage of each is not realized until adolescence. They emphasize, as do the earlier chapters, the very real need for rich experience in play and work, with plentiful concrete materials, in pre-primary and primary school life. And they illustrate for us the way in which logical thinking gradually approaches its abstract form.

At first this power of reasoning logically demands great mental effort, so it can only be applied for short periods at any one time.

CHAPTER FIVE
Classification and seriation

Logic is closely interrelated with mathematical thought. In our primary schools today we are recognizing this fact. We are also recognizing that logical thinking should, in itself, be fostered. We are encouraging children, through the sorting out of materials, to exercise their developing powers of classification, seriation and other logical processes in the probing of problems that are as closely related to all the incidents of everyday life and of play as they are to mathematics and logic. As we examine these problems, we see that the solutions to many of them depend basically on the skill to classify and the skill to seriate. These two skills, according to Piaget in his book *The Early Growth of Logic in the Child*,[1] are the two roots of logical thinking that are the first to develop in the human being.

In this chapter we report on typical responses of young children to a few of the tests for diagnosing the stages of development of the skills of classification and seriation, that Piaget devised and that we repeated with Lancashire children.

I CLASSIFICATION

Piaget sees the skill of classification as developing in three stages. The first of these stages he calls 'Pre-classification', the second he calls 'Quasi-classification' and he recognizes only the last one as true 'Classification'.

The materials he uses in diagnostic testing are mostly geometrical 'cut-out' shapes that will be seen in the photographs that follow but a few are toys and, at Stages II and III, words.

---

[1] Subtitled 'Classification and Seriation', Jean Piaget & Bärbel Inhelder; Routledge & Kegan Paul. All references in this chapter are to *The Early Growth of Logic in the Child* except where otherwise stated.

Stage I — pre-classification

At this first stage a child cannot sort out objects into classes at all. If asked to 'sort out all these things', whether they are toys or shapes, he lays them out in a pattern that has, for him, a satisfying visual (or Piaget says 'graphical') appearance. Perhaps instead of a pattern it is a picture. In either case Piaget calls it a 'graphical collection'. Certainly it is a 'collection' and not a classification. Perhaps the child strings the objects in a line, matching each object to the one before it but varying the criterion by which he compares as he passes from one pair to the next. And yet such a child is just beginning to classify in his general thinking as he struggles to build up language, for language is dependent on classification. With adult help he can put his trains on one shelf, his cars on another and his books on a third. His very use of these words involves something in the nature of classification: but he would not consciously think out such a classification. Piaget puts great stress on the influence of 'good visual form' being stronger than that of words or of consideration of criteria at this stage.

Stage II — quasi-classification

With most children this stage begins about the time they first enter primary school, and lasts for about two years.

As the prefix 'quasi' suggests, these children seem to be able to classify and, in the very simplest sense of the word, their collections are an early form of classification. But none of the subtle niceties of classification is being observed.

Such children can, approximately, sort elements out into their major classes, for example, into squares, circles, triangles and strips (long rectangles); but they are still mentally dragged towards the idea of pattern and so they may have two or more groups of any one of these classes. But, even when they achieve separation into major classes, they cannot cross-classify, nor can they see small classes within large classes, e.g. they cannot subclassify red, blue and yellow triangles within the class of triangles: yet, if they are asked to do so, they can reclassify according to colour.

They cannot think concurrently of a whole class and of a part of a class. Piaget gives examples of children being unable to say whether a bunch of mixed flowers had in it more flowers or more tulips. Another group of infants could not decide whether a string of wooden beads had more wooden beads or more red wooden beads.[2]

Such children often cannot see that classes are contained within other classes in the sense of a hierarchy, e.g. black baby

[2] Jean Piaget & A. Szeminska, *The Child's Conception of Number*, Chapter 7.

ducks < black ducks < ducks < birds that swim < birds < creatures.[3] Put into adult words, this would read 'Black baby ducks are a category of black ducks, which are a category of ducks . . .', etc., or 'There are fewer black baby ducks than black ducks . . .', etc.

Perhaps most difficult of all, they cannot deal with what Piaget calls 'intensive' and 'extensive' attributes. For example, an intensive attribute of cats is that they 'miaow' — for all cats, and only cats, do so. An 'extensive' attribute is that they have fur: all cats have fur, but so do dogs and rabbits.

They cannot classify according to negative criteria.

Finally, at this stage, there is still a tendency to try to classify an object according to its use rather than its properties.

Other complications include the duality principle, the class of one and the null class.

Only a few of these niceties of classification, that develop during Stage II and that are present at Stage III, will be dealt with further in this chapter.

Stage III — true classification

During the course of junior-school life, most of the complicated skills of classification, mentioned above as missing from Stage II, are acquired. The purposely vague diagram on right shows the sequence in which the skills tend to mature. On the age axis of the diagram specific ages have not been written in, since variations can be very great from child to child. The diagram is only intended to show the sequence in which the skills tend to develop.

From the diagram one point of particular interest that stands out is that cross-classification (by a matrix) can be seen to develop in three stages. A very young child, perhaps as young as five years, can often *solve* a matrix more quickly than an older child can. During the next three years or so he will begin to be able to *build* one. Both of these activities are heavily dependent on the child's relying on 'good visual form' — a characteristic of pre- and quasi-classification. Then, during the rest of his junior school or early secondary school life, the real ability to cross-classify (by *foreseeing* a matrix) will develop. This demands reliance on the mental effort of true classification. It is interesting to notice that, because he no longer relies on the immediate impact of visual form, he waits to think and is therefore not so adroit at solving a matrix as a much younger child might be. This apparent reversal of ability is often the key reason for unexpected results when children between the ages of about four and twelve compete in puzzles of a matrix nature.

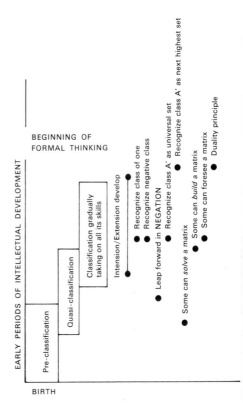

Sequence in which early abilities in logical thinking develop.

Note: In mathematics 'not A' is always written 'A'.

---

[3] < is the mathematical sign for 'is smaller than'.
  > is the mathematical sign for 'is greater than'.

It is often worth warning adults that it is unwise to try to hurry a child who waits to think and unwise to be critical of an older child who does not solve a matrix as quickly as another child of an earlier stage does.

The examples that follow show the reactions of three Lancashire children to the test on separation of major classes. The youngest sister, Nicola, was presented with an assortment of coloured geometrically shaped discs and asked to sort them out. The elder sister, Tricia, was allowed to watch but was asked not to join in until Nicola had finished. A third sister, Alison, who is not photographed, waited until last and so had ample time to think what she would do.

STAGE I*b*: Nicola pounced on the shapes, exclaiming, 'Oh! Lovely colours!'

She immediately started building them into aesthetically pleasing patterns.

After a few minutes we stopped her and said, 'Nicola, now could you try to sort them out so that the discs that are alike are all put in one place, and others that are alike are put in another place?'

We discussed 'helping mother tidy up the toy cupboard' by putting dolls on one shelf and books on another and puzzles on yet another: Nicola joined in this conversation. We held a similar discussion about putting away cups and saucers and plates. Then, 'Now could you do the same with those discs?'

Nicola went back to them, slightly influenced towards classification according to shape or colour, but much more influenced by the 'good visual form' of the pattern she was producing. Time after time she changed the development of her pattern, sometimes seeming to categorize by shape and at other times by colour. As one looks at the pattern, from her left to her right, one sees that she started with squares. The corner square was pink: next to it she put a related pink triangle and rhombus. Then, unrelated to either, came a paler pink triangle: related to this she put on top of it a white triangle: this was followed by a related white trapezium, below and above which she built three more trapezia. She seemed, for the moment, to have got under way with classification by shape. But then the effort was too much for her and the other discs were put down, carefully and painstakingly, just where they looked pretty.

All this time she was talking volubly and enthusiastically. She had produced an excellent example of a graphic collection with nearly every object matched to the one before it, but with the criteria varied from one pair (or occasionally one trio) to the next. She was considering the aesthetic value of the pattern as a

48

Nicola. A graphic collection.

whole but, as far as classification by criterion was concerned, she could only consider adjacent discs at any one time.

STAGE II: Since Nicola's elder sister Tricia had been watching Nicola's effort we took great care to ask her to see the problem differently. Quite clearly one of us asked, 'Tricia, could you sort them out quite differently from the way Nicola sorted them? Remember what we said about putting plates and cups and saucers in different piles on the shelves.'

'Yes!' said Tricia, 'and spoons and knives in the drawers.'

'Well! What are you going to take notice of in sorting these?'

'Shapes and colours.'

'Good! Now will you sort them?'

Very soon Tricia had started collecting the group of equilateral triangles and the group of trapezia, but the latter broken into by one triangle. In spite of our reminding her at intervals 'not to

49

Tricia. Quasi-classification.

bother to make them into patterns', but only to 'put together discs that are alike', she still persisted in aiming at good visual form. The biggest pattern, hidden in the picture by her hands, consisted mostly of isosceles triangles but also had a trapezium in it.

At this point we stopped her and asked her to tell us the names of the shapes, and she gave names to them all: 'Triangles, those four-sided things [rhombuses], stars, squares', etc.

'Could you put all of one shape into one pile?' she was asked. 'I have,' she said.

Then, 'Could you make piles of different colours without bothering about shapes?'

Tricia managed to do this alternative classification.

Obviously we could not hope for her to achieve a subclassification nor a cross-classification. But when it came to the question of hierarchical classification she was immediately correct in putting down the following sequence: 'Black Ducks: Ducks: Birds that Swim: Birds: Living Creatures', although in the next problem she put the hierarchy as: 'Boys: Big boys: Boys and Men: People.'

STAGE III: The eldest sister of the three, Alison, immediately corrected this last hierarchy. She also placed the discs into a matrix with shape as one co-ordinate and colour as the other. Alison had unambiguously abstracted the criteria of colour and shape and so reasoned logically that she could classify two ways at once.

We did not test any of these three children on 'extension' and 'intension',[4] nor on classification by negation, but an interesting example of young children's difficulty even in just putting themselves into a negative category can well be quoted here.

A student had a class of six-year-old children, most of whom would have been likely to be at Stage II in the development of the skill of classification as described above. They were clearing up before going out to play, so the student thought it a good moment to issue letters to some of them to take home to their parents. As soon as he had quietened them he said, 'I have letters for some of you to take home. Will you put up your hands if you have NO elder brothers or sisters in the school?'

Most children put up their hands and he distributed the letters. Then came a break, during which time a stream of children trickled back to him saying something along the following lines: 'Please sir! I took a note because I have got an elder brother. You know, Johnny! He says I don't want the note.' Or, 'Please! I didn't take a note. I haven't got a brother or sister. But Jane hasn't got one either and she took a note.'

This sort of difficulty in one of the niceties of classification is what makes the process of development from Stage II to Stage III in classification slow enough to last right through junior-school life. Equally important is the fact that, only by giving a child plentiful practice through tasks in which he can exercise these developing skills, can a parent or teacher ensure that the child's power of logical reasoning will have a firm foundation on which to mature during adolescence.

True classification is a potent intellectual tool once it is firmly developed.

II SERIATION

Many psychologists would claim that all through our lives we recognize differences before we recognize similarities.

Yet, at first, it often seems to adults that seriation should be more difficult than classification. Piaget has found that the two skills develop in any child more or less concurrently, or, if there is any difference, seriation develops slightly earlier than classification.

The essential link seems to be this. We have seen that young children begin their first classificatory efforts by sorting objects into 'good visual form' (graphic collections). Similarly, a series lends itself to good visual form. Further to this it does not present complicating difficulties such as 'intension' and 'extension'.

Seriating thus demands no more ability than classifying, and good visual form has the same, or perhaps a stronger, motivating effect on the child.

As early as about eighteen months old, a child can use Montessori nesting-boxes to build a tower with descending sizes of boxes. Similarly, with very little difficulty, he can pack the boxes into one another. This is certainly the beginning of seriation but, as with pre-classification, it is dependent on a sensory-motor schema rather than on forethought. It is by implanting such schemas in himself, through play, that a child lays a substructure for seriation and hence for logical thought.

There is a difficulty here. The easiest objects to seriate are graduated rods such as Cuisenaire rods. Yet the pre-school child is genuinely unable mentally to 'conserve' length (see p. 13 on the difficulty of conservation in general) so, in the very act of trying to seriate lengths, the child is also forming the concept of length at the same time. It is generally just before entering school that he becomes fascinated by the act of measuring things against one another. Soon after this he will try to seriate them. But, as with classification, he can only concentrate on any two adjacent rods at one moment and he cannot consider a series as a whole.

Hence, at this stage, Cuisenaire rods are doubly valuable. It is probable that the plentiful use of these rods in the first two years of schooling encourages children to pass rapidly through this first stage (of being able to compare only adjacent rods) and on to the next stage at which they begin to recognize uniform differences in a short series. Through laborious measuring to achieve a Cuisenaire 'staircase' and repeatedly gazing at the finished pattern, a child sees the uniformity of differences in the configuration. Concurrently the pattern of lengths helps him achieve a concept of length.

Seriation of rods with increasing differences offers a slightly greater challenge but this, too, is soon mastered.

It is important that, concurrently with his experience with Cuisenaire rods, a child should have ample experience in seriating not only other geometrical shapes but also such objects as toys or plants or people.

In the development of the ability to seriate there is a period of what Piaget calls 'semi-anticipation' of a series. This has no parallel in classification.

Piaget carried out many and varied tests for seriation, of which only the most simple and straightforward are illustrated by photographic examples later in this chapter. His three best known are the following:

Problem A

He asks the child to seriate two separate sets of ten rods of increasing length (i.e. twenty lengths) and then to intersperse them correctly. The test could equally well be carried out with any similar shapes of increasing area or of increasing colour intensity or of any other increasing factor. It is important to remember, however, that the very young child may not yet have conserved length or area or whatever the factor may be that is under consideration.

Piaget himself, in carrying out this test, found children at the following three stages:

STAGE I: The pre-school child generally cannot seriate even the first ten rods (or shapes, colours, etc.). Perhaps he cannot even seriate three or four of them. If he can seriate a few he will form several subseries and then be unable to link these subseries together.

STAGE II: Most children of infant-school age have a general idea of what is asked of them in this problem but they can only achieve seriation of each ten by trial and error. Also, if the separate series are arranged for them, they have the same difficulty when, by trial and error, they try interspersing.

STAGE III: A junior school child generally starts work more systematically. Very soon he will start by looking first for the largest or smallest, or both, to place in position and then for the largest or smallest of those that remain. He may or may not work from both ends. This shows that he has an understanding of $A > B > C$, etc., or $E < D < C$, that he has anticipated the series and that he is working from a plan that he has formed mentally and not by trial and error. He will intersperse the two series equally systematically.

No photographs are published here of children doing this, but the difficulty one child had in making an initial series can be seen in the photograph illustrating an attempt at the following problem.

Problem B [5]

An interesting and slightly different test shows an apparent, but not real, discrepancy from the results of problem A.

The child is presented with a jumbled series of a few dolls. He is also given a jumbled series of coloured 'walking-sticks' of varied lengths, together with pencils of the same colours as the sticks. First he is asked to arrange the dolls in a series and, if necessary, helped to do so. Then he is asked to draw the series of sticks that would suit the series of dolls and, after that, to arrange the actual sticks in similar order to the dolls.

The apparent discrepancy comes when a child, at a middle stage, proves unable to seriate the actual sticks but yet has been able to

[5] Jean Piaget & A. Szeminska, *The Child's Conception of Number*, Chapter 5.

William.

draw the series of sticks with the right gradation of lengths
(perhaps giving them the wrong colours). He is, in fact, being
led strongly by 'good visual form'. Piaget calls this stage (of
correct pencil drawing only) the stage of 'global anticipation'. It
is because of this global anticipation that the discrepancy is
apparent and not real. It is preceded by a stage of complete
inability to solve the problem and followed by a stage of 'complete and analytic anticipation'.

The following is an example of a child at the stage of 'global
anticipation'.

William was unable to seriate seven soldiers correctly, but the
photograph shows that he has achieved two subseries which
could not be linked because one subseries was falling and the
other rising. One soldier he could not place, so he abandoned
him. As for the sticks, he made two clear mistakes in matching
them to the soldiers in this unseriated line, since there was no
'good visual form' to guide him. But a test on an unseriated line
of soldiers is more difficult than was intended: William only
attempted this at his own wish.

Once he had been helped with seriating the soldiers he drew the
series of sticks, that he anticipated giving them, in correct
sequence of lengths, but he was still only partly successful in
distributing the actual sticks.

Problem C.

The third problem in seriation that Piaget applies is that of forming a matrix in seriation. He calls this 'multiple seriation'. The
photographs that we reproduce are of children attempting this

54

problem, using twenty-five similar triangles of five sizes and of five intensities of blue in each size.

Because the stages expected are parallel to those for classification, it seems unnecessary to list them in advance of the examples.
STAGE I: Damaris merely enjoyed making patterns with the triangles.
STAGE II: Derek was first given only five triangles of different sizes and of equal colour intensity and he seriated them almost immediately. His method began as trial and error but his correction of his errors was so quick that it seemed very probable that he soon had an anticipatory schema in mind.
When faced with the twenty-five triangles he found the problem immeasurably greater. The photograph shows his final result but this was achieved with a certain amount of adult help, in the form of encouraging leading questions, and after twenty minutes of hard work.
Derek started by using his first series of five, all of the darkest blue. Then he started on an isolated series of the palest blue but he was distracted from this when he suspected that the smallest of the pale blue should go beyond the lower end of the dark blue.

Damaris. Pre-seriation.

Derek. Early seriation.

Derek solving a seriation matrix foreseen and built by Alison Jacqueline.

Then he started hunting for smaller ones among the other intensities of blue, which, after a lot of alterations, resulted in a series of five small triangles ranging in colour. This led him to seriating the four remaining large ones similarly.

It is of little value to go through all the moves that followed but, just before the photograph was taken, he had, of his own accord, achieved the pattern now shown with (a) one colour subseries out of sequence, and (b) just two or three triangles out of size-sequence. These were pointed out to him with the simple question: 'Are you satisfied with where you have put that colour?' or, 'Do you think that triangle is in the right place?'

Each time he saw his error and corrected it.

STAGE III: Alison Jacqueline had been watching Derek and had had time to think, so she was quick to make the matrix shown in the photograph. Derek watched and admired.

56

As soon as Alison's matrix was completed we sent Derek away while we collected five triangles from random places in the finished matrix. Derek returned and was able easily to replace these five triangles in their correct places, thus demonstrating Piaget's claim that quite a young child can solve (as contrasted to anticipate) a matrix because of the help given by its visual form.

Concluding statement

It would be impossible to sum up the whole of this chapter in a few sentences. Perhaps just a few words extending what it has contained would serve a better purpose.

Firstly, it illustrates again the Piagetian theme of early experiences forming a basis for intellectual growth and of further continuous experiences enriching that growth. Where the foundations of logic are concerned, assimilation of sensory-motor experiences in extreme youth culminates in a 'logic of action' involving relationships (classification) and correspondences (seriation) which are a substructure for the future operation of logical thought.

Piaget mentions the place of language in this development. Words inevitably force a beginning of classification and occasionally of seriation too but, in seriation, form seems to have a greater effect than words have. Nevertheless, language helps to accelerate both classification and seriation, and to bring them to perfection.

Piaget's analysis is a slight variation from the 'Gestalt' theory that perceptual knowledge exists before all else or from Bruner's theory that perception is, in itself, an act of classification.

There is no doubt that Piaget has shown us that unambiguous abstraction of criteria in classification and seriation makes inference possible. Inference is essential to logical reasoning.

The chapters that follow will deal with the course that this logical reasoning takes.

CHAPTER SIX

The development of an ability to recognize one's own contradictory statements, in solving a problem, and to correct them

From the time when a baby first plays with a toy duck in his bath he is launched on a study of the science of floating and sinking which will lead him into developing the skills of classification[1] and of the elimination of contradictions. Gradually, as he grows through primary and early secondary-school days, experimenting in floatation will lead him still further into forming concepts of volume, weight, density and specific gravity.

Piaget has studied the stages of self-contradiction that a child passes through in the process of this learning and has classified them into the usual three stages with substages. Unlike his other studies quoted in this book this study demands no ingenious apparatus but only a large bowl or two of water and the obvious variety of objects to be floated or sunk. At Stage III it is necessary that two (or more) of these objects should be identical in shape and volume and that one of these two should be heavier and the the other lighter than its own volume of water. In the examples that follow, we used a hollow, plastic box that had contained a toothbrush and identically shaped bars of wood and of metal, in an otherwise random variety of further objects.

The Piagetian stages[2]

STAGE I*a*:[3] Before about four years old, few children can predict whether objects will sink or float, partly because, in their minds, objects do not conserve their properties over a period of time. These children can consider only one object at a time. It is hardly possible to test them for contradictions in their reasoning, as they expect an object to float or sink according to their own whim of the moment rather than because of the properties of the

---

[1] See Chapter Five.
[2] From Jean Piaget & Bärbel Inhelder, *The Growth of Logical Thinking from Childhood to Adolescence*, Chapter 2.
[3] Jean Piaget, *The Child's Conception of Physical Causality*, Chapter 6.

object. If, under pressure, they do give explanations, these can be as wildly contradictory as:

'The toy soldier sank because it was red,' immediately followed by: 'The ball floated because it was red too.'

STAGE I*b*: This will include early infant-school life, and during this stage a child will attempt to classify floaters and sinkers but will generally fail to do so. He is satisfied with multiple explanations as to why his results are not what he anticipates, and he is oblivious of his own contradictions as he flounders to explain first his predictions and then the reasons why particular ones prove to be wrong. These children begin to think in terms of heavy things sinking, but they confuse 'big' with 'heavy', thus laying the foundation for plentiful contradictions.

STAGE II*a*: The child makes a real effort to remove the main contradictions as he moves towards realizing that sinking is due to RELATIVE, rather than ABSOLUTE, weight. This is a tremendous mathematical advance, as it is the beginning of a concept of a relationship. The child is beginning, none too clearly, to make a double-entry classification and to realize that sinking or floating depends on all four interrelationships between weight and volume; but he himself has, as yet, no fully developed concept of either weight or volume.

Hence he will probably use the word 'heavy' whether he means heavy or of high density, because he is only intuitively aware of the fact that these are two separate properties.

Nevertheless, this move towards a use of class-inclusion is a milestone in the skill of classification and comes about partly as a result of his attempts not to contradict as he classifies.

STAGE II*b*: A child begins to be able to put into serial order[4] weights that are of the same volume, or volumes that are of the same weight, and this is the dawning of the idea of specific gravity. Yet he is still not at all sure of the conservation of volume. Hence he tends to compare the weight of an object with the weight of *all* the water in the vessel, rather than with the weight of the water displaced. Consequently, although at Stage II*a* he began to make a conscious effort to eliminate contradictions, at Stage II*b* he still cannot manage to do so.

STAGE III: This cannot be reached until the child is capable of formal thought, for two reasons: (*a*) The complete concept of volume itself involves proportions and so cannot be expected until formal thinking is reached. (*b*) The weight of water displaced cannot be *seen* but only realized as the result of hypothetical thought.

Hence, Stage III is a generalization using hypothetical thinking, of the comparisons that were attempted empirically at Stage II. At Stage III contradictions are, at last, eliminated.

---

[4] Serial ordering is another basis of logic. See Chapter Five, and Jean Piaget & Bärbel Inhelder, *The Early Growth of Logic in the Child*, Chapter 1.

Derek, Stage Ia, trying to sink a boat.

The examples that follow illustrate the confusions that cause the contradictions described above and the gradual growth of logical thinking that disperses these confusions.

STAGE Ia: Derek played with the toy boat happily for a time, floating it in many directions. Then he decided to sink it. He pressed it to the bottom and expected it to stay there. His explanations of what he was attempting next were too fragmentary to be coherent but amounted to a statement that, with the hose, he was now putting the water on top of the boat. This attempt proved to be great fun and lasted for ten minutes or more: then Derek abandoned the boat and turned to other play with the hose.

Derek knew that a stone would sink and predicted that a tennis ball would sink too. When he was asked to explain why, in fact, the ball floated, he said contentedly: 'Because I put it there.'

Obviously Derek had no basis for sorting objects into potential floaters and sinkers and this is typical of Stage Ia.

STAGE Ib: Rosanne was asked to predict about each of the objects separately.

'Will this red ball float or sink?'

Rosanne: 'Float' — and when asked why, she hesitated and then said, 'Because it's round.'

'So will this penny float?' (and 'why?').

'Yes! 'cause it's little.'

'What about this wooden button?'

'It will go down.'

Demonstration showed that it floated and for this Rosanne gave as her reason that it was small too. Asked for any further reason, she said it was because it was blue.

'Will this blue plastic box sink?'

Rosanne: 'No! It will float.' It did. So why?

''cause it stays on top.'

We started on a further sequence.

'Look, this piece of stone sinks. I wonder why?'

Rosanne: ''cause it's big.'

'But this plastic box is bigger and it stays on top. Why?'

Rosanne: 'Yes! But it's not stone.'

'Then why did the stone sink?'

''cause it's heavy.'

'But when you go swimming you float and you are heavier than the stone.'

Rosanne: 'I'm not.'

We were defeated for the moment; then we tried once more.

'Will this pencil float or sink?'

Rosanne: 'It will sink.'

'It's floating. I wonder why?'
Rosanne: ''cause it's long.'
'Because it's long! Any other reason?'
Rosanne: 'It's shiny.'
'So what will happen to this strip of shiny metal?'
Rosanne: 'It will go down.'
Rosanne, through play experience, had learned something about what will sink and what will float. But when it came to attempted explanations, she was quite unaware that she was contradicting herself.
STAGE II*a* PROGRESSING TO II*b*: Jill predicted most of her 'floaters' and 'sinkers' correctly but her statements of her reasons were not always completely logical. According to her predictions:
A spoon would sink, because it was heavy.
A plastic cup would float, because it was light.
A wooden ruler would float, because it was 'mostly wooden'.
A ring of Scotch tape would sink, because it was heavy.

Rosanne, Stage I*b*, guessing wildly why things float.

Jill, Stage IIa, puzzled as to whether heavy wood could sink.

These predictions proved to be true.

A shallow metal tray faced her with more of a problem. She expected it to sink, because it was heavy, but it floated. Why should this happen? She tried several more times and managed to sink it by putting it in on edge. So why did it sometimes sink and sometimes float?

'Because it is heavier now that it has water on it.'

After this she was very puzzled about a large block of wood and a smaller, but heavier, stone. She predicted that both would sink, because they were heavy, then quickly corrected her thinking with:

'No! I'm not sure, because wood floats.'

After being pressed to make up her mind, she decided.

'Well! It's a heavy bit of wood, so perhaps it will sink. I'll try.'

She had to try in the sink because the wood was so large. She was not very surprised to find her estimate about the wood to be incorrect. When asked what she thought the explanation might be she replied: 'Well! It seemed heavier than the stone, but perhaps that was because it was in my left hand. It can't really be as heavy. Or is it just that the stone and the spoon sank because they are heavy for such little things?'

A few days later Jill came back, having tried out, of her own accord, a series of little things of approximately the same size and seriated them in weight approximately accurately. She laid them out in order, saying:

'This end is the lightest and that the heaviest. See, the milk bottle top floats, the wooden button floats, the penny sinks, and that stone sinks with a plonk.'

'Would the stone have sunk with such a plonk in a whole sink full of water?'

Jill puzzled for a moment or so and then answered doubtfully, 'No! Perhaps not. Oh! Was that why the heavy wood floated in the sink?'

In the few days of self-imposed active exploration, Jill had matured from Stage IIa to Stage IIb. But she was still far too young to use the hypothetical thinking necessary at Stage III.

STAGE III: Susan immediately sorted all the objects correctly, except that she was puzzled about the wire and the very fine steel wool. Ultimately she categorized these correctly too. Then the questioning began.

'Why do you think the wooden spoon will float?'

Susan: 'Because it is wood. All those wooden things will float.'

'Why?'

Susan: 'Because all wood has little pockets of air inside it.'

'And those metal things that you say will sink. Is it the same sort of reasoning?'

62

Susan: 'Yes. Metal things are heavy, so they sink.'
Up to this point the answers might have been illustrative of Stage II, but here the break into Stage III really came as a result of the question: 'Then why did you expect the steel wool to float?'
Susan: 'Because it was really steel wool puffed up with air. Look. If I screw it up tight, it will sink.' She demonstrated.
'Why did it sink when you did that?'
Susan: 'Because it remained just as heavy as before but took up much less space, so it could press through the water better. I mean it could displace the water. Look! Now it is fluffing up again so it will float.'
'What did you mean by "displace"?'
Susan floundered a little in her explanation so it was suggested to her that she might illustrate her argument with the three identically sized and shaped bars of wood, metal and hollow plastic.

Susan, Stage III, puffing up steel wool to float it.

Susan: 'These are all the same volume. The steel one is very heavy for that volume, so it sinks and presses its own volume of water out of the way. The wooden one half sinks so it presses half of its volume out of the way. The plastic one is full of air so it stays nearly on top and hardly presses any water away.'

There were no contradictions in Susan's arguments and her concepts of volume and of displacement were secure.

Concluding statement

Children's reasoning, before they reach adolescence, can be very insecure even when they are dealing with problems and with the concrete material that should help towards a solution. Often they cannot recognize that they are contradicting their own earlier statements. Still more difficult is it for them to recognize that unexpected practical evidence contradicts their own suppositions. Not until adolescence can they safely hypothesize as to why these contradictions occur, and it is well into adolescence before they can prove or disprove their hypothesis about such contradictory evidence.

As usual, this constant challenge in concrete reasoning gives them pre-logical experience. Something as simple as constant play in water provides a happy and generally unnoticed way of promoting intellectual growth.

CHAPTER SEVEN

The development of the operation of reciprocal implication in young children's mental development[1]

(Observation of children's reaction, at successive ages, to the problem of setting the path of a billiard-ball.)

This is one of the simpler tests devised by Piaget for testing the stages of development of a line of problematic reasoning in young children. Through what stages does a child pass in developing the ability to see an implication and to work out the reciprocal of the implication?[2]

Children of about the age of seven years can often recognize when angles are of equal size, although, certainly, they find it more difficult if the arms of the angles are the paths of moving balls rather than visible lines. Nevertheless these same children, when faced with the problem of hitting a target with a re-bounding ball, do not foresee that the solution is to aim at equating the angles of incidence and of reflection.[3] They must reach the age of formal reasoning, in early adolescence, before they can do this. Their struggles at intermediate ages are very revealing.

Piaget's apparatus for testing children's reactions to the problem consists of a board, surrounded by buffers, with a spring 'gun' pivoted at one corner. Children can aim a ball in almost any direction in their attempts to make the ball hit the buffer and rebound on to a target.

STAGE I: In all the children Piaget tested, he found that the very young ones just try empirically, by trial and error, to make a hit. They are concerned with success or failure, but do not consider the means of attaining success. They consider the starting-point and the target but they pay little attention to which part of the buffer must be hit. Even if they hit the target, they never examine the path that the ball takes to find out why a hit was scored.

---

[1] Chapter prepared by Norman Ellis, Mary Sime and Anthony D. Todd.
[2] Jean Piaget & Bärbel Inhelder, *The Growth of Logical Thinking From Childhood to Adolescence*, Chapter 1.
[3] The advanced mathematical thinker knows that this is not strictly accurate, but inaccuracies are so slight that they could not be registered on such simple apparatus.

STAGE II: In late infant-school and early junior-school life children employ concrete reasoning. They begin to relate the point of rebound with the path that the ball takes after the rebound, generally, at first, considering that it is the position of impact that matters without seeing that this varies with an angle. They think in terms of distances rather than angles. They may get a 'vague global intuition' of the equality between the angles but they cannot see that equal angles are an essential need. Nevertheless, they are beginning to see that a certain action implies a relevant result. But they cannot see how, as a result of this implication, to estimate backwards from the desired result to the necessary initial direction of hit.

STAGE III: This stage is not reached until the age of formal thinking. At Stage II the child has succeeded in isolating all the elements needed in the law, and now he sets out to formulate the law by looking for what conditions are not only present but also necessary. He asks the essential question concerning implication: 'It happens repeatedly that the angles of incidence and of reflection are equal. Does this imply, reciprocally, that I can only get the right rebound angle by creating an equal angle of incidence at a right point?'

He then sets out to demonstrate that this is so.

The following are actual examples of these three stages.

STAGE I: Fiona's response was typical of Stage I. She shot with gay abandon and real enthusiasm, and with no specific idea as to which of the targets she was aiming at. Most frequently she missed them all. When she hit a target she was overjoyed but she did not show any sign of having learned from her experience why the last ball had hit. She tried to do exactly the same again (and failed) but did not give any sign of trying to apply her success in hitting one target to the problem of hitting another.

Fiona, Stage I, shooting at random.

Jane, Stage IIa, estimating buffer position by distances.

STAGE IIa (using a simpler version of the table): From her very first shot, Jane was conscious of the fact that the point of rebound of the ball from the buffer was of crucial importance to the result. She selected such a point, took very careful aim at it, shot and missed, through her ball passing to the left of the target. She remarked, 'Oh! It went too far that way. So I must aim further this way.'

She proceeded with this sort of reasoning, about the points to aim at on the buffer, for several more shots. Once she hit the ultimate target but she could not repeat it. When questioned, she made it quite clear that she was calculating her measurements to the right and left of the last position hit on the buffer to match the distances by which the ball missed the target.

When further questioned about the importance of the point of rebound she said, demonstrating with her hand, 'Well, you see, it is the angle that matters'.

Q. 'Which angle?'

A. 'This one' — showing bewilderment at her gesture, seemingly, not being understood.

Q. 'Is there any other angle that matters?'

A. 'No! The others all missed.'

Q. 'Did the ball that you hit with only make one angle?'

A. 'Yes! I want to get it again.'

Jane had reached Stage IIa, since she was, in a systematic way, serially ordering her points of impact on the buffer and co-ordinating them with the hits and misses. But she was not

67

beyond Stage II*a*, since she did not even look for the reason for their relationship. She saw no implication of such a relationship. She was persisting in dealing with *facts*, whose accuracy was due to serial ordering and to correspondence, but she could not attempt an explanation in formal terms. She was unaware of the implication of the angle of incidence creating an equal angle of rebound.

STAGE II*a*–II*b*: Harvey was at the particularly interesting point of just reaching Stage II*b*. He was exploring all possible operations, with the use of the materials to help his reasoning. He was quite sure that the point of impact on the buffer was of real importance, if the target was to be hit. But his only reference to angles was, 'It doesn't come off at a right angle.'

He announced that he would aim at a point on the buffer halfway between the table end and the target and then said in a puzzled tone, 'It misses by four inches!'

Soon after this session of testing Harvey reached Stage II*b*, as depicted by Alison in the next example.

STAGE II*b*: Alison, after a few tries, managed to hit her target and, when asked to explain her success, she said, 'I made a V to there, and then, when it didn't hit, I tried a little further this way.'

Harvey, Stage IIb, explaining that the angle is not a right angle.

On being further questioned, however, she showed that she did not appreciate the equality of the angles that she was drawing with her fingers, though she saw them as angles 'that mattered'.

STAGE III: Dorothy was at Stage III and able to reason out her plan of action formally. She marshalled most of her facts (at first ignoring the differences of perpendicular distances from the buffer) by taking one or two trial shots. She said, 'The direction it goes in it comes off in.'

Then, remembering some school learning, she said, 'Oh! The angle of incidence equals the angle of reflection.'

As a result of this reasoning she then, at first, began to consider that she would obtain the correct angles by aiming half-way along the appropriate point of the buffer. She saw that this method missed the target because of the differences in perpendicular distances, corrected her calculation accordingly, and, with great confidence, took careful aim and hit her target. Similarly, she hit each target in turn.

It may be said that this test was hardly valid because of Dorothy's knowledge of the law from previous teaching. Many of the

Alison, Stage IIb–IIIa, drawing equal angles without realizing their equality.

Dorothy, Stage IIIa, able to estimate the angle of incidence.

Piagetian tests cannot be used, for this reason, to see how reasoning develops naturally in older children: they can, however, be used for a teacher to decide whether a child understands such a law, before giving the child further work dependent on that law.

Concluding statement

As usual, the slowness of the transition from the haphazard trial-and-error methods of Fiona to the reasoned formal thinking of Dorothy is something that few of us realize until it is brought home to us by some such vivid demonstration as this. The laborious learning that goes on, through exploration with such materials, in the junior-school years is again emphasized. And this skill, of seeing implications and of looking immediately for the necessary reciprocities, is an essential tool that must be developed before Euclidean geometry can be started.

Section C:
Patterns of Mental Activity in
Logical Thinking

INTRODUCTION

In this section we continue with examples from the only one of Piaget's books[1] (with co-author Inhelder) that examines at all fully the changes in logical thinking which take place as a young person passes from true childhood into adolescence and develops the skills of thinking formally (i.e. by use of abstract formulae) and of reasoning hypothetically. 'Formal thought reaches its fruition during adolescence. The adolescent, unlike the child, is an individual who thinks beyond the present and forms theories about everything, delighting especially in considerations of that which is not.'[2] Piaget frequently refers to formal thinking as if to a goal that is to be reached: the delightful book, *The Moral Judgment of the Child*, devotes the last and very long chapter to it, making it the focal point of the whole study. The 'essay', as the authors call *The Growth of Logical Thinking . . .* (and it is interesting to remember that the true meaning of the word 'essay' is 'attempt') helps us to see, at last, the whole intellectual growth of the young person as a continuous, rounded-off process.

It also tries, scientifically, to analyse and contrast the mental structures which characterize the thinking of the children at the stages of Concrete Operations and Formal Thinking.

In this last section, we introduce examples (from Part I of *The Growth of Logical Thinking*) in which a child at the stage of Concrete Operations struggles through a 'quasi' pre-development of propositional logic in an empirical way and only achieves true propositional logic on reaching adolescence and the stage of Formal Thought.

In Chapter Eight we examine one more such example as we have had in Section B, but a more difficult one. How soon can a child

Is it really true that children can't think logically until 12/13 - if that's the case why teach Maths/science as they invoke logical thought processes.

[1] Jean Piaget & Bärbel Inhelder, *The Growth of Logical Thinking from Childhood to Adolescence* subtitled 'An Essay on the Construction of Formal Operational Structures'.
[2] Jean Piaget, *The Psychology of Intelligence*, p. 148.

see that, when there are many variable factors in a problem, only one of these can be tested at a time while the others must be held constant? And at what stage can he discipline himself into organizing the isolation of the factor to be tested? To test each he needs experience in negating some of them. In Chapter Nine we deal with negating. As a child tests these factors he accepts some as operative and negates others. Through what stages does he pass in reaching the ability to negate?

This leads right on to the need to examine the growth of what Piaget and Inhelder call 'operational schemata of formal logic', to which they devote the second section of the book. And so our last three chapters illustrate the 'operational schemata of formal logic', or, in other words, the paths that our mental activities take (perhaps at the speed of lightning) as we solve a problem. Three of these schemata are dealt with here. Like the simple schemata of early childhood, referred to in Chapter One, they can, when roused, trigger off mental activities as dynamic as concepts. These patterns of mental activity can be compared to patterns of mathematical form. Outstanding among them are the three illustrated here. One can be seen as a dynamic form of the mathematical 'Klein 4 Group', in which we weigh factors against one another, within the total group of factors involved, and without altering the total group. We choose a point of identity, then we negate, or we reciprocate, or we combine both of these factors by correlating them. Thus, mentally, we discipline ourselves into studying the proportions of a problem within the problem itself. By what stages do we develop this ability? This is the theme of Chapter Ten.

But there is another mature mental schema, by which we operate on problems through evaluation by geometrical proportion. This is dealt with in Chapter Eleven, by examining children's development of thinking about sizes of shadows.

Lastly, how do we decide what all the possible combinations of factors are in a problem that we might examine, and work on in the two ways mentioned above, in order to find out which one, or which ones, of the combinations give a solution? We do this by forming a mental 'lattice' of the possible combinations. This 'lattice' is illustrated in Chapter Twelve. Piaget brings in terms such as 'structured whole' and 'combinatorial system', for which the more serious student would do well to refer to the original book. A slender introduction to this systematic combinatorial system is dealt with in the final chapter, by repeating Piagetian tests in which children were asked to experiment with colourless, odourless liquids until a reaction produced colour. Only by having a systematic mental plan of action, from which one can extract and examine every possible hypothesis, can one find a solution to a problem that can in no way be explored by any of the senses (sight, taste, feeling, smell or touch) until a right solution brings colour and therefore confirmation by sight.

To sum it up, this section brings to a climax the Piagetian view of the relationship between logic and psychology. It claims that 'Logic may be applied as a theoretical tool in the description of the mental structures that govern ordinary reasoning'[3] and it demonstrates empirically the long slow path of growth that these structures take in their development before reaching maturity in most people in either early or late adolescence.

---

[3] Jean Piaget & Bärbel Inhelder, *The Growth of Logical Thinking from Childhood to Adolescence*, Introduction, p. viii.

CHAPTER EIGHT

Development of the ability to separate the variables in a problem and to hold all except one constant while testing that one[1]

The experiential learning of mathematics that is penetrating our primary schools today is relieving many a secondary school-teacher of having to cope with the disheartening appeal from teenagers, 'Sir! I can do the ordinary arithmetic. But can you show me how to do problems?'

How, in fact, does the ability to solve problems mature in the course of early mathematical experience? There are many lines of development that contribute to its maturing: one of the chief of these is the gradual emergence of an ability to consider all the possible varying factors in a problematic situation and then, systematically, to hold all except one constant, while testing that one, and then to proceed, similarly, with each of the others. It is generally right at the end of junior-school days, or early in secondary-school life, that the complete ability to do this is attained.

The stages of development of this ability are shown clearly if one confronts children with a problem,[2] devised by Piaget, that seems boring to many adults but holds most children enthralled. The reasoning it demands is mathematical although the sub-ject-matter is physics.

Children are confronted with a board over which, at a height of about an inch, six metal rods are clamped in such a way that each, or all, of them can be shortened to any fraction of their length. Only one end is clamped and the other end left free. The rods are of two or three materials (brass, copper, steel) and of two or three shapes of cross-section (round, rectangular and square) and there are two thicknesses for certain shapes. Discs of varied weights can be fixed to the free ends of the rods. The children are confronted with the problem of finding out which of the five variables (weight, length, material, shape,

[1] This chapter was prepared by Deryck Weston and Mary Sime.
[2] Jean Piaget & Bärbel Inhelder, *The Growth of Logical Thinking*, Chapter 3.

thickness) influence the possibility of a disc pressing down the end of a rod until it touches the board.

Children who were being educated in a variety of Lancashire schools were encouraged to attempt this problem and the following are examples of the results obtained. As usual, they are listed under the Piagetian stages that they illustrate.

STAGE I: At this pre-operational level, the child's explorations are unorganized. He makes random attempts at putting on weights, and talks about results, but offers no scientific explanations of them.

STAGE IIa: The child begins to search for cause and effect. He begins to seriate such factors as thickness or length of rods, or even to report which rod bends most or least: yet, to quote Piaget, he gives answers that are 'not as they might be selected with the question in mind'.[3] In other words, his explorations are still random and his observations are statements of his interest.

STAGE IIb: The child uses what Piaget calls 'multiplications between asymmetrical relations'.[4] This sounds complicated but it merely means that the child might, for example, record that a long thick rod bends as freely as a short thin one. The essential difference between this stage and the next one is that at Stage IIb the child still only experiments by trial and error, rather than doing so from a hypothesis.

STAGE III: At this stage the child begins to make an attempt to form a hypothesis and to set out to verify the results. At the first substage he cannot organize this attempted verification effectively, but by Stage IIIb he can plan his experiment so that each variable is tested in turn while all other variables are held constant.

This holding constant of all variables but one is one of the fundamental skills in good adult reasoning.

Piaget compares the mental pattern of possibilities that is held in reserve to a mathematical 'lattice'. The mental actions of exploration on the isolated variable he compares to a mathematical 'group'.

STAGE I: Janet began by playing with the rods, flicking or pressing them with her fingers and ejaculating when they sprang upwards on release. With encouragement, she began to fix on discs and to report such facts as, 'Look! It is touching.'
Q. 'Why is it touching?'
A. 'Because I put that on it.'
Q. 'Would it have touched if you put this smaller one on?'
A. 'Yes!'
She put the smaller one on a different rod, which did not touch. Her only response to this was, 'Oh!'

[3] Jean Piaget & Bärbel Inhelder, *The Growth of Logical Thinking*, Chapter 3, p. 50.
[4] Jean Piaget & Bärbel Inhelder, *The Growth of Logical Thinking*, Chapter 3, p. 51.

Undeterred, she went on playing.

STAGE IIa: At first Denyse was completely bewildered by the large number of variables, and she tried putting on weights and lengthening and shortening rods seemingly at random. Her first obviously premeditated action was to test the full length of the thin, circular-sectioned, copper rod with the medium-weight disc and to find that it touched the base. Then she shortened the rod until it did not touch the board. (The disc remained hooked on throughout the shortening.) Then she said, 'It does not bend enough now that it is short.'

Q. 'Did it bend enough when it was long?'

A. 'Yes! It touched.'

Q. 'What do you learn from that?'

A. 'That being long helps.'

She did not aim at confirming this with other rods but she soon shortened all the rods to the length remaining on the copper rod and tested them in sequence with all the discs. None touched. She then lengthened two at random, put the lightest weight of disc on one of them (thin, circular, brass) and the heaviest on the other (thick, square, steel). Neither touched. She reversed the discs and the thin, circular, brass rod touched. She repeated this several times and then said, 'Look! This touches with this one.'

Q. 'What do you learn from that?'

A. 'That that one is stronger.'

It took half a dozen more reversals of discs before she ejaculated, 'Oh! Weight matters. Length matters and weight matters.'

She did not see that this could have been proved with only one rod, i.e. she had not planned, mentally, the holding constant of all but the one variable of weight; in fact, she seemed worried because the heavier weight did not also hold down the thicker, square, steel rod. As in the case of length, she had achieved her result by trial and error and by the chance holding constant of the other variables. Neither did she manage any further result although she played with the apparatus at intervals throughout the afternoon and evening.

Denyse was at Stage IIa. She was, at least, systematically trying out each variable in turn, although she was oblivious of the other variables confusing the results. She was also systematically registering her results. She was beginning to classify. And she was serially ordering the lengths of rod that she tested and the sequence in which she put on weights. But she did not yet see the problem as a structured whole.

STAGE IIb: Robert carefully adjusted a thin and a thick rod to the same length and predicted that the thin one would bend to touch the base but that the thick one would not. His prediction

Janet, Stage I. Random testing.

Denyse, Stage IIa, testing for the influence of length, but with different weights on rods of different materials.

Robert, Stage IIb, holding constant the variables of length and weight only.

was, in fact, correct, but not valid, because, although he was careful to use the same weight on each (and was sure that a heavier weight would also bend the thinner rod), he did not consider the fact that the rods he chose were of different materials. STAGE IIIa: Christine and Vivienne enjoyed a session of hypothetico-deductive reasoning before setting out to verify, by experiment, whether they had reasoned a right answer. This formulation of a hypothesis, preceding an attempted verification, is typical of Stage III. But they were only at Stage IIIa. They managed to eliminate all variables except length and so demonstrate that length was influential by gently drawing a rod through the clamp, with a weight on it, and watching the weight rise. Similarly they hypothesized that a heavy weight would flex a certain rod, while a light weight would not flex the same rod: they verified this. They tried, but failed, to isolate and test the properties of thickness and of cross-section.

Christine and Vivienne. Hypothetical discussion.

STAGE III*b*: It is not until the age of formal thinking that one can form an all-over plan by which to hypothesize, in turn, that each of the variables may influence flexibility and then to isolate each variable and test it.

Sally formed such a mental plan at once. We asked her to give a running commentary of what she was doing and it began like this:

'Well, there are five variables (metal, length, weight, shape of cross-section and one other . . . oh! size of cross-section). I'll test them all, because it could be any of them. I'll start with that last one, thickness.'

For this she selected the two circular copper rods, at full length, and found that the lightest weight of disc made each of them touch. Systematically she shortened them both, equally, a few inches at a time, until she reached a point where the thin circular rod touched the base under the lightest weight but the thick circular copper rod did not.

79

'Yes!' she said, 'Look, cross-section makes a difference.'
'Can you explain?'
'Yes! Everything else is equal, they're both copper, both circular, both the same length, and I used the same weight, and only the thin one was flexible enough to touch. I've also proved that length counts, because the thick circular copper rod touched under that weight when it was long and it doesn't now.'
Similarly, she went on to isolate and test the other variables.
The logical thinking involved in this Stage III*b* approach is typical of the good formal thinking needed in much mathematical work.

Concluding statement

The simple conclusion to be drawn from this experiment can be put in the form of a warning. We, as adults, often fail to solve a complicated problem because we have failed to isolate each variable factor in the problem to examine it. Certainly a child before the period of formal reasoning should never be expected to find the solution to such problems, although, given sufficient concrete materials, the junior child will get some way towards the answer. But he cannot manipulate these variables mentally at the same time: therefore he cannot plan a course of action by which to do so practically. Piaget would say that he cannot 'form an experimental schema'. This does not imply that he will not enjoy and benefit from puzzling over such problems if the variables are few and the materials for solving them are adequate.
Piaget uses this experiment as an example of what he calls 'feeding' information into a 'combinatorial system', or into a 'structured whole' (i.e. all the possible combinations of all the variables), and forming propositions mentally about possible answers. One then sets out to prove or disprove each such proposition.[5] We speak of it as the schema of 'All other things being equal'. Words like 'disjunction' creep into his explanation, and the use of 'disjunction' (e.g. 'sometimes short rods bend and sometimes they do not. Why?') is a difficult and an adult skill. But it is essential to hypothetico-deductive reasoning.

[5] See the next chapter, on negating.

CHAPTER NINE

Elimination of negative factors in solving a problem

In everyday life we meet many problems to which we find a quick and satisfying solution, while accepting calmly that an alternative solution might have been equally satisfying. Often we do not trouble to investigate whether or not that alternative suggested solution could be a correct one.

To what extent do our minds normally react this way? How possible is it for young children to build schemata on wrong assumptions because of this tendency not to isolate and eliminate negative factors in a problem?

Although Piaget's test for exploring how far children eliminate negative factors has been well publicized on television, it seems right to study it here as it is a fundamental logical skill. The skill of absolutely rejecting negative factors must be seen as a contrast to the different skill of temporarily holding them constant, which was dealt with in the preceding chapter. Both skills require the child to hold constant variables other than the one that he is isolating for testing at the moment. The contrast lies in the fact that in the flexibility problem (Chapter Eight) he needed to test each variable in turn, holding the others constant, and he found that each is positive: in contrast, here, with the pendulum, he also tests each in turn and he finds length a positive factor. Then he faces the more difficult task of demonstrating the other factors to be negative.

The child is asked which of the variable factors (length of pendulum, terminal weight, height of drop or impetus of 'push') influences, or influence, the rate of oscillation. All the material aids that he might want, for example a metronome or stop-watch and writing materials, are available.

Janet and Jane. Stages I and IIa.

The stages through which children pass in reaching the ability to solve such a problem can be numbered in the usual way:

STAGE I: Early infants generally show themselves to be quite pre-operational in that they tend to see the rate of oscillation as completely dependent on their own actions. Piaget says their 'physical actions still entirely dominate their mental operations' and they 'fail to distinguish between these actions and the motions observed in the apparatus itself'.[1]

STAGE II: Most junior children are clearly aware that there are variables in the apparatus itself that might influence the frequency of oscillation. They can enumerate these variables. They can, in fact, seriate each of them and can record the frequencies of oscillation at each testing. But they cannot isolate these variables, except that of impetus (i.e. their own 'push'). Their tests are still completely empirical.

STAGE IIIa: This is a very interesting stage, for what Piaget calls 'a crude form' of formal operations is now present. The child can separate out the factors if the adult presents him with two factors of which only one is variable, but he himself cannot produce such combinations. He is groping towards forming a systematic plan of action but cannot at present organize it mentally.

STAGE IIIb: At this stage, he can separate out the variables and exclude the inoperative ones.

The following examples illustrate the above-listed stages:

STAGE I AND IIa: Jane was very clearly at Stage II, perfectly aware that the pendulum could be adapted to swing faster or more slowly by altering a variable in the pendulum itself or possibly by altering her own 'push'. She explored, by trial and error, altering sometimes the length, sometimes the height of drop, sometimes the weights, sometimes her own push — but with no clear-cut plan of action, or systematic elimination of the variables that were ineffective.

By contrasting a very short pendulum with a very long one, she came to her decision: 'Look! It's the length that matters.'

Janet (Stage I), squatting on the floor and sucking her thumb in her anxiety, said repeatedly, 'Push it harder! Push it harder! Push it quickly.'

Jane replied contentedly, 'No! Look! It slows down' — quite oblivious of the fact that this statement was not quite accurate but yet sure that the impetus was not the solution.

Having decided that variation in length influenced the rate of oscillation (though not having demonstrated it by holding other factors constant) Jane was satisfied to pass on to other interests. On later occasions she came back to swing the pen-

[1] Jean Piaget & Bärbel Inhelder, *The Growth of Logical Thinking from Childhood to Adolescence*, Chapter 4, p. 69.

dulum again, though more from fascination and to substantiate her decision than to probe further into the problem. At no time did she set out to show other factors to be ineffective.

This is an interesting example of a correct statement being made (after experimentation) by a very young child, of the child being absolutely convinced about her true factual answer and yet not having explored the greater part of the problem: it is, in fact, an example of a right answer for an inadequate reason.

STAGE II*b*: By trial and error in lengthening and shortening the string, Alex managed to get the pendulum ticking in synchronization with the metronome and said, 'It's the length that counts.'

When pressed hard to say more she could not do so; the idea that length of pendulum was in inverse proportion to rate of ticking was still beyond her. Yet she was obviously serially ordering the lengths as she listened for the ticks — empirically — and that was enough to place her in group II*b*.

Alex took no notice of the length of arc through which the pendulum was swinging and so neither acknowledged nor rejected that as a possible influence. Again, when asked directly whether weight made any difference, she said contentedly, 'No! It is the length.' And so she made no effort to acknowledge or exclude it.

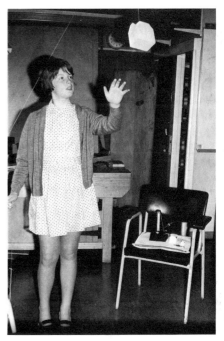

Alex. Stage IIb.

Although the above response would fit Alex clearly into Stage II*b* she seemed, by her long periods of silent thought, to be attempting to make a formal mental plan. She was at an age when formal operations were becoming possible in a general way and it was clear that she could not be hurried in such thinking. She was, therefore, offered a week to work out the problem and to bring in a written reply. The following resulted.

Alex's diagram.

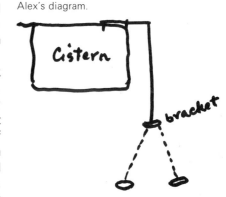

Her written answers covered several pages of an exercise book so cannot be reproduced fully. They were dated, in diary form, and showed that she had had the problem in mind intermittently right through the week. Having been convinced already that it was 'length that counted', she had watched for examples of pendula in everyday life, culminating with a chain (on a cistern) that had been lengthened so that small children could reach it and had been stayed half-way down by a wall bracket. Although she could not be explicit in the following statement she was influenced, in her thinking, by the fact that this stay had been put in to stop the chain swinging too widely: she could not quite separate this out from swinging too fast. She did not, at any time in this solo investigation of the problem, time-test any of the pendula that she watched for but yet was satisfied in confirming her previous conviction that length was an operative factor. This instinctive desire to worry-out the

83

solution mentally, which, in itself, probably delayed progress towards a possible correct demonstrable answer, was an excellent illustration of the tenacity in thinking which accompanies the intellectual development of a change from concrete reasoning (i.e. from the example to the solution) to hypothetical reasoning (i.e. from the hypothetical solution to the testing of an example) that dawns in most children of about thirteen years old.

Unfortunately, Alex ended by accepting from an adult the wrong information that 'weight counts too'.

STAGE IIIa: Christopher was at the point that Piaget would call 'a crude stage' of formal operations.[2] He could test one of the factors when either an adult or chance isolated it for him but he could not form such a plan himself. Further, he responded easily to the implied suggestion that, having ascertained that length was an operative factor, he needed to examine the other factors as well and either accept or reject them.

The easiest of the five factors to explore was length, since, for this, Christopher only needed to pull or to slacken the retaining string. He did this until the pendulum 'ticked' in synchronization with the metronome: he seemed unaware that he was holding the weight constant purely by chance and that he was dropping from random positions.

'Look!' he said, 'I've done it.'

'How did you manage it?'

'Well! By getting the length right.'

'Does the place you drop from make no difference?'

'Oh! I didn't try dropping from different places. I will try dropping from the edge of the mat and then from further back here where I am putting this brush.'

Quickly, he lashed the string to a support while he fetched and laid down the brush.

Oblivious of the fact that he had been 'dropping it from different places' all the time and that he had now fixed the length of the string, seemingly for manual convenience, at the same interval as he had last used, he proceeded to try very long and very short drops. He found that the pendulum still synchronized with the metronome and announced that the position of dropping made no difference. He gave the pendulum one vigorous push.

'Neither does push!' he said, 'Look!'

'Have you tried changing the weights?'

'Oh! No! It might, mightn't it?'

He changed the weight, leaving the length still conveniently tied as before, seemingly by chance, and said, 'Now, look, I will drop the heavier weight from the same point. There! I knew it

[2] Jean Piaget & Bärbel Inhelder, *The Growth of Logical Thinking from Childhood to Adolescence*, p. 73.

Christopher. Stage IIIa.
(Photograph taken by Lyn Mayer.)

wouldn't make any difference. It's just the same as with the other weight. It's only length that you have to alter.'

So, at last, he had shown signs of holding a factor constant but it was a factor that he had already eliminated as inoperative. Was he, we wondered, holding length constant intuitively? Someone asked, 'Why have you left the string tied at that length for so long?'

'Because I went to fetch the brush,' he replied.

'And what is your final answer to the problem?'

'You just have to make it longer for a slow tick and shorter for a quick one. And that's all.[3]

---

[3] It is encouraging to realize that Christopher, in his approach to this problem, showed himself to be at a stage quite normal for his age in spite of the fact that, throughout school life, he has had to struggle against dysgraphia.

Kate, Stage III, calculating length of pendulum needed for a special rate of oscillation.

STAGE III*b*: Kate and Permjit found no great difficulty in isolating each factor in turn, to test it, while holding the others constant each time. Immediately they found that the longer pendulum oscillated at a slower rate than a short one. Possibly they knew this anyway, theoretically, but, if they did, they had not digested the fact thoroughly enough to foresee, at first, how to slow down the metronome to a convenient starting speed. So it seemed the test would be valid as contrasted to being an examination of learned facts.

They worked completely cooperatively so it was unnecessary to record the separate contributions of each to the solution. The positive solution of the influence of length had been easy for them. The exclusion of the negatives was more difficult and it was some time before they had formulated and carried out a plan of action which was this:

They set up the metronome (with help) at a convenient speed and purposefully tied the pendulum to oscillate at that speed, dropping the weight from various heights and noting that it made no difference to the speed. With the same weight on they pushed from those same heights and recorded that there was no change in speed. Then they changed the weight and dropped and pushed again from the same heights. It made no difference.

Permjit and Kate, realizing that a metronome is based on the principle of an inverted pendulum.

Then they went through the whole process again with a longer pendulum. Of course, the results were similarly convincing.
It was impossible, at this point, for us to resist a searching question, 'Have you learned anything about a metronome?'
'Oh! A pendulum upside down!'

Concluding statement

It has been revealing to examine how easily a child jumps to conclusions about a positive factor and ignores the existence of negative factors. This leads us to ask two rhetorical questions:
1   How frequently do we, as adults, take it for granted, like the child at Stage I, that our own personal actions are of prime importance in an even weightier situation, when, in fact, they are not so?
2   How often are we easily satisfied that we have the whole and only answer to a problem when we have not, in fact, taken care to eliminate the possibility of further solutions?

CHAPTER TEN

The development of children's patterns of thinking seen through exercises with a balance. The Klein Four group pattern[1]

In primary schools today, we are accustomed to seeing children weighing their rabbits, weighing themselves, weighing and spilling rice and sugar, and we accept, blandly, that they are 'learning through experience'.

How often do we consider the precise path that such experiential learning is taking?

In *The Growth of Logical Thinking*,[2] Piaget has guided us in studying the steps through which the full understanding of equilibrium and of proportions matures. He claims that the actions involving the reciprocities, negations and correlations in the moving of weights on a balance not only illustrate the INRC[3] mathematical group, but also set up an activity pattern in the child's own thinking that is an internalized INRC group. The simple questions that he asks children about weights and about positions of weights on the arms of a balance force the question of proportionality. In sequence we see children coping with identity, then with reciprocity, then with negation and ultimately, in early adolescence, with correlativity.

In the work recorded here children, ranging in age from four and a half to twelve years, were tested along Piagetian lines and some of their responses, quoted below, illustrate the results that Piaget leads us to expect. They are:

[1] Chapter prepared by Harvey Long, Betty Pennington, Mary Sime and Kenneth Worrall.

[2] Jean Piaget & Bärbel Inhelder, *The Growth of Logical Thinking*, Chapter 11; see also pp. 318–20 and Chapter 17 for further study.

[3] The Klein Four group, known also as the INRC group from the initial letters of the words Identity, Negation, Reciprocation and Correlation (or Correlativity). To remind readers whose mathematics is stale: A mathematical group is a group of interrelated mathematical activities (in this case four) known as elements. These elements can be made to interact with one another internally within the group, changing the internal pattern or structure of the group without in any way changing its total value. Of the elements, one is always identity (the first activity). Every element in the group has its inverse. Any two elements acting together necessarily produce a third which is already a member of the group: hence the group is what is called 'closed'.

STAGE I*a*: A child fails to distinguish between his own actions and the objects he can control. He may achieve a state of balance by distributing weights at random.

STAGE I*b*: A child understands that, to achieve balance, weight is needed on both sides and even that the weights should be approximately equal (which is the starting-point for the idea of reciprocity) but he cannot proceed towards equalization in a systematic way. Nor does he interrelate weights with distances, except in an intuitive way.

STAGE II*a*: Although weights are added and then subtracted (negation) exactly and distances are compared and, by trial and error, are made symmetrical, there is nothing more than intuitive regulation in co-ordinating weights with distances. Also, the child does not know how to invert weight/length relations from one side of the balance to the other.

STAGE II*b*: A child is now working towards the law of proportionality in that he realizes that there is some sort of inverse correspondence between weight and distance (a starting-point towards correlativity) but he is achieving his results by examples that are too inexact for him to establish the law. His measurements are what Piaget calls 'qualitative' as contrasted to 'quantitative' or 'metric'.

STAGE III*a*: A child now discovers the law and understands it clearly enough to explain it.

STAGE III*b* (not illustrated below): A child discovers how to achieve a required slant on the arm of the balance and thus moves towards an understanding of 'work' in the mathematical (or physics) sense.

The following were our results:

STAGE I*a* APPROACHING I*b*: When Nicola approached the balance the arm was horizontal with no weights attached.

Nicola, Stage I, exploring at random but with a sense of wonder.

The cups were at the ends of the arms. The following is an extract from the conversation and activity that ensued:

Q. 'If we put a weight on this side [left] what will happen?'

A. 'It will drop.' (Obviously meaning the left side will drop.)

Q. 'How can you make it level again?'

A. 'By pushing it up.' She did so. She seemed surprised when it did not stay and tried repeatedly.

Q. 'Can you do it without pushing it with your hand?'

After a little thought Nicola put a weight in the right-hand cup and so produced a state of balance.

Q. 'If I put two more weights on this side [left], like this, what must you do to that side [right] to make it level again?'

A. 'Add a weight to this side.' She did so and, finding it still unbalanced, intuitively added another.

As a response to further similar questions, with ever-increasing numbers of weights on one side, Nicola went on adding weights, one by one, to the other side without any forethought about how many to add to achieve balance. Nicola did not, at any time, consider the 'negation' of taking a weight off again to achieve it. Nicola's first responses were at Stage I*a*. With all the egocentricity of early childhood, she saw herself as the only agent to achieve equilibrium and she expected the apparatus to respond to her actions. But she was on the brink of Stage I*b*, for a simple question led her into finding (by trial) that weight was needed on both sides, though she did not consider the need for equal weights on both sides. Nor was she at all concerned with the distances of the weights from the axis.

Through these activities Nicola was absorbing the experience of reciprocity although she was not yet understanding it enough to think about it clearly. Piaget would say that she had not yet 'abstracted' the idea of reciprocity. She was still not quite at Stage I*b*. She did not attempt to achieve balance by the action of 'negation' (i.e. taking off the weight that had been put on).

STAGE I*b*–II*a*: Deborah could manage all that Nicola ultimately managed and she also thought of attaining equilibrium by taking off the weights that had been put on (i.e. technically, by negation). After this the interview proceeded as follows:

Q. (with the arm horizontal and empty cups at both ends). 'If I put these two weights in this cup and one weight in the other side [left], is there anything I can do to get it level without adding or taking off any weights?'

A. 'Move the cup nearer the middle.'

Q. 'Which one?'

Deborah was obviously not sure which one. By chance she got it right at the first attempt but she was sufficiently intrigued

by this to try it on the other one as well. On being asked several other similar questions, she made a variety of attempts, seeming sure that movement of position was the clue but being unsure of which cup to move and whether to move inwards or outwards. By trial and error she always succeeded in the end. (This is merely a further example of reciprocity, as she was compensating fixed weights with positioning.)

Q. 'Now that it is level, with one weight in this cup at the end and two in this other cup half-way along, what will happen if I put another weight in the cup at the end?'

A. 'It will stay the same, because there will still only be two weights in it, the same as here.' On finding that the left side did, indeed, drop, she moved the right cup (with its two weights) outwards and obtained balance. (There were now two weights in each cup.)

Q. 'Now, if we put another weight in the left cup, what else must we do to keep it balanced?'

A. 'Move the weights on this side [right] towards the middle.' She did this and, finding that it gave a greater imbalance, she moved the left cup inwards, too, and achieved balance. She continued like this, always achieving her aim in the end but never being able to estimate in advance what to do.

It is during Stage Ib that operations often start to form which counterbalance weight with distance but the interest of the child is generally only in one property at a time. Deborah illustrated this. She seemed to be anxious to keep symmetry in the distances: Piaget often points out how children of this age tend to go for a 'good visual form'. She struggled unsystematically to keep reciprocity in two separate ways, (a) by having approximately equal weights on each arm and (b) by having equal distances — but she kept the two symmetries separate. She negated in two separate ways, (a) by taking off what had been put on, and (b) by moving inwards what had been moved out — but, again, she was unsystematic and she saw the two negations separately. But she was overlapping into Stage IIa in that she showed an intuitive knowledge that weight and distance were, in some way, interrelated. She was becoming more systematic in her reciprocating and negating.

STAGE IIa–IIb: Christopher was successful on all the tests for reciprocity and for negation. He was then introduced to the balance when the arm was horizontal with one weight in the cup on each extremity. The following is a typical extract from the testing that followed:

Q. 'If we add another weight to this [right] side, what will happen?'
A. 'It will drop.'
Q. 'How can we make it balance again?'
A. 'Put one in the other side [left].'
Q. 'Could you keep it balanced without adding weights or taking any off?'

Christopher, Stage IIa–b, intuitively co-ordinating weight with distance.

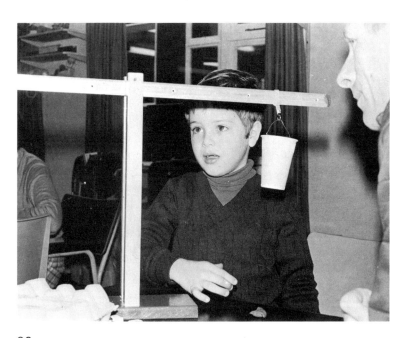

92

A. 'Move the cups on both sides towards the middle.' He tried this several times and ultimately said, 'It won't balance.'

The balance was then put in equilibrium for him, with cups at the ends and three weights in each.

Q. 'If we add two more weights to the right-hand side, what must we do to keep it level?'

A. 'Move the left cup towards the middle.'

Christopher was at Stage IIa, in that he was successful in all the tests for reciprocity and for negation to the extent of looking for exact (as contrasted to Deborah's approximate) weights and distances. His method of finding distance was still by trial and error. He was intuitively co-ordinating weight with distance. Although he systematically chose the exact opposite movement to the one that was needed the fact that he was consistent showed that he appreciated that there was a rhythmic connection between weight and distance but he could not see what it was. This was drawing him towards Stage IIb. He certainly showed no sign at all of inverting weight/length relations from one side of the balance to the other.

STAGE IIb: Martin could equalize the balance without any difficulty, by adding or subtracting weights. He was also quite sure about the direction in which he needed to move objects on either arm to compensate for unequal weights. The following is one example:

Q. 'I am now putting one weight on the right-hand side and two on the left. Can you balance it without adding or removing any weights?

A. 'Yes! By moving the heavier weight towards the middle.' He did so quite firmly. Although weights were added and subtracted several times, Martin moved the positions accurately each time and refused to be shaken in his certainty that a heavier weight must be moved nearer the axis to counterbalance a lighter weight.

Martin had seen that the relationship of length to weight is inverse. But he had to find his exact position by trial and error, since he was still only seeing the relationship 'qualitatively' and not 'quantitatively'. He could compensate added weights on one side of the balance with movement outwards on the other side — again, only qualitatively.

STAGE IIIa (Alison Jacqueline): The balance was in equilibrium with one weight at the end of each arm. Alison was asked:

Q. 'If we add one more weight to the right-hand side, how can we obtain balance again?'

Alison immediately added another weight to the left-hand side. Before the next question that weight was removed.

Q. 'Can you do it without either adding or removing a weight?'

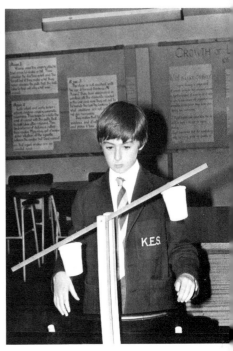

Martin, Stage IIb, sure of everything except the exact position.

93

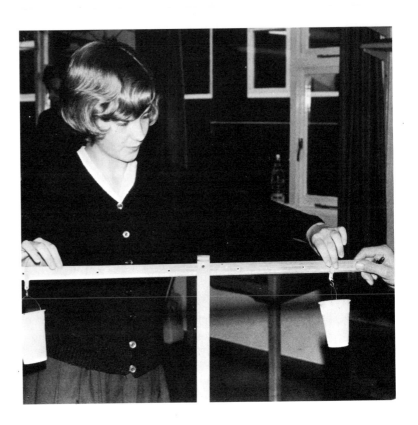

Alison Jacqueline, Stage III, moving firmly
as a result of calculation.

A. 'Yes! By moving the weight on the other side half-way
towards the middle.'

Q. 'Why?'

A. 'We have put twice as much weight here [right] as we have
there [left], so we have to move these weights half-way towards the middle to make up for it.'

Alison responded equally well to further such questions, all of
them with simple proportions.

Alison fully understood how to apply the laws of equilibrium to
solving this problem and felt safe in her theoretical knowledge
to the extent of stating a clear plan of action before carrying it
out. She could consider the interrelation, at any one moment, of
the addition, or removal, of weights on one arm and she could
either reciprocate it on the other arm by identical action, or
could correlate it on the other arm by bringing into action a
change of position to compensate it. She could do this on either
arm that she chose. And she could calculate the exact distance
to compensate the alteration of weight so long as the proportions were simple. Alison could thus implement the whole
INRC group mentally, which is typical of Stage IIIa. This does

94

not mean, however, that she understood the INRC group theoretically as a person at Stage III*b* would do.

Concluding statement

What these illustrations show is basically two things: (1) that although very young children can seem to understand the process of weighing, it is not a full understanding, and (2) that the development of this understanding is extremely slow and complicated. If we ask a five-year-old to 'weigh' how many bricks counterbalance a toy car, let us not suppose that he understands what he is doing. Nor does a six-year-old, who equalizes flour and sugar on the two pans of a balance preparatory to cooking a cake, understand the weighing process. Both are getting valuable experience but it would be wrong to say that either can weigh. When the pan of sugar drops lower than the pan of flour it is quite an experience for a young infant to decide which pan to add to: we can train him, mechanically, by showing him but this is no more a true education than training him to the tricks of addition before he appreciates numbers. He can only teach himself by repeated experiences of trial and error until he begins to appreciate the reciprocities. And taking something off a pan to get equilibrium is not always so obvious as putting something on: let us be patient about that point.

What about apparatus? It would seem from these illustrations that balances with fixed pans are the best to begin with, so that the simple compensations of weights alone can become clearly understood without variations of distances blurring the picture. Then, very soon, the equalizer will become a useful tool for introducing the second variable of distance. Here, again, we must be careful not to try to force an apparent learning, too soon, of 'two rings on number three equals three rings on number two', and so forth.

It is not only in the infants' schools that science apparatus, involving equalization, is so necessary: it is needed throughout the junior school for the experiences of compensation to be gained and, indeed, it is needed in the early secondary school. The balance is the simplest of these tools to help us learn about equilibrium, proportionality and so forth. What are the others? This question is one of the very big challenges to the junior-school teacher.

Through such experiences the child gradually develops not only an understanding of the scientific principles involved but also the habit of examining the proportions of a problem within the problem itself. The 'group' pattern of mental activity thus set up matures into an 'operational schema' and into a 'formal concept'.

CHAPTER ELEVEN

Where is your sense of proportion?[1]

All of us have asked that question at some time or other and we have all implied by it that we considered the person whom we were addressing as unreasonable or making some unreasonable suggestion or deduction at that moment.

Most of us who, in studying developmental psychology, watch the growth in young people of an ability to think logically are mildly surprised when we first realize how fundamental to logical thinking is the skill to see the factors of a problem, truly and mathematically, in proportion to one another. It also comes as a still more startling revelation when we realize that this crucial skill develops only late in junior-school life, even when only concrete problems are involved: we are more prepared to realize that a young person is well into adolescent years before he can evaluate proportionately abstract ideas connected with, for example, justice or ultimate good.[2] In studying any Piagetian theme we become accustomed to seeing that, in the development of a skill, plentiful reasoning in solving the concrete problems evoked by primary-school experiences are a necessary foundation for the use of the same skill in the abstract and hypothetical thinking of adolescence and of adult life. This is as true in the application of a sense of proportion as it is of any other mental process.

Earlier chapters (e.g. Chapter Ten) have reported on Piaget's studies of children's development in appreciating proportion from the point of view of equilibrium.[3] We now turn to the similar, but not identical, ability to appreciate proportions of a geometrical nature which is revealed very clearly if one applies the shadow tests devised by Piaget and reported in *The Growth of Logical Thinking*.[3] Reference must first be made to Piaget's earlier work on children's understanding of the formation of the shadows themselves.

[1] Chapter prepared by Fred Jones with Mary Sime.
[2] In *The Moral Judgment of the Child*, Piaget studies the sense of proportion shown as a child matures from an enthusiasm for egalitarianism to an appreciation of equity.
[3] Chapter 13.

In these earlier books he has shown us that most children of pre-school years do not realize that a shadow is caused by an object interrupting light, so there is no value in questioning them about the proportions of sizes of objects and their shadows.[4] In a later work[5] he shows us that during pre-infant and infant-school days this understanding develops and it is soon followed by an ability to predict the approximate shape of shadow that will be thrown by any simple form of object at whatever angle that object is tilted (for example, a tilted circle throws an elliptical shadow).

But to test on the problem of the proportionate size of circular rings and their shadows, it is essential that the shadows should themselves be circular. Piaget takes the precaution of using the following simple apparatus: it consists merely of a series of wire circles on 'stalks', a light and a screen. A board, joining the light and the screen, has holes bored in it at regular intervals.

Through what stages does a child pass in discovering the law that the sizes of shadows cast by the rings are directly proportional to the diameters and inversely proportional to the distance between the rings and the light?

STAGE I: Very young children will not respond to these tests by considering proportion at all.

STAGE IIa: Children discover that a larger circle throws a larger shadow from any given position than a smaller circle would throw. They do not look into the question of 'How much bigger?' And they discover that distance plays a role in determining the size of shadow.

STAGE IIb: Children know how to construct inverse correspondences but they prefer direct ones and so they calculate from the screen rather than from the light.

STAGE IIIa: A child is definitely thinking in terms of proportion but he is not quite sure about what proportions he is dealing with. He sees that shadows are dependent on divergent light rays and so he begins to measure the distance of each ring from the source of light. Not until Stage IIIb does he see these light rays as forming a cone. Nevertheless, at IIIa he has discovered proportionality and that it is inverse. But he cannot generalize to all cases. He is satisfied by having demonstrated a single case.

STAGE IIIb: He can generalize the above to all possible cases, and so can formulate and apply the law.

STAGE I: Derek's response to questions about shadows was, at least, entertaining. He was riding his tricycle and the conversation went as follows:

Q. 'Derek. May I take your photograph?'

[4] Jean Piaget, *The Child's Conception of Physical Causality*, Chapter 8.
[5] Jean Piaget & Bärbel Inhelder, *The Child's Conception of Space*, Chapter 7.

Derek, Stage I, playing with his shadow.

A. 'Yes! — And my tricycle?'
Q. 'Oh! What is this dark mark on the path?'
A. 'It's my shadow.'
Q. 'How did it get there?'
A. 'I don't know.'
This question was pressed home in several ways and he insisted that he did not know. Then he was asked:
Q. 'Is it always there?'
A. 'No! When the sun comes out.'
Further similar questions got no better response but he cycled in circles, watching his shadow as he did so. Then,
Q. 'Look! I have a shadow too. It's bigger than yours.'
A. 'Yes!'
Q. 'Do you know why mine is bigger?'
A. 'No!' But he shows interest.
Q. 'Why do you think it is?'
A. 'I don't know.' — He still shows interest.
Q. 'Could I hide my shadow?'
A. 'No!'
Q. 'Look! I've hidden it in your daddy's shadow. How did I do that?'

98

A. ''cause you did *that*' — he came and joined the line, 'Mine's gone too!'

Then he skipped off again.

Q. 'Could I hide mine in yours?'

A. 'Yes! You come over here.'

A game started up of jumping on heads of shadows. After a few moments, Q. 'Could you jump on your own shadow's head?'

A. 'Yes!'

He tried to do so for a full ten minutes. Then he said he would 'try tomorrow'.

As a parting shot, he shouted, 'I'll tell you when I can.'

Derek was at Stage I rather than at a possible Stage 0 for he was at least interested in shadows. As is described in Piaget's earlier books, he did not associate them with an interruption in a source of light. As far as proportion is concerned he did not consciously show any understanding of 'big people:big shadows', although he may, intuitively, have been aware of such a relationship.

STAGE IIa: Jane was the first to be tested on the conventional materials. She was immediately interested in the question of 'Which ring will make the biggest shadow?' and stated that the biggest ring would do so.

Q. 'Could you show me by fixing the ring into these holes in the wooden rod?'

Jane, Stage IIa, fixing the ring by trial and error.

She fixed them in, one behind the other, showing no regard for position. By chance the biggest circle cast the biggest shadow.

Q. 'Will the biggest ring always cast the biggest shadow?'

A. 'Yes.'

Q. 'Will it always cast the same size of shadow?'

A. 'Yes' — but the tone of her voice suggested doubt.

Q. 'Would you like to move it about to make sure?'

On experimenting Jane soon discovered that the size of the shadow could be varied but it was some moments before she sorted out whether to move the ring backwards or forwards to enlarge the shadow. At last she began to make steady firm movements along the full length from the screen to the light and back again. She was absorbed in doing this for a long time. Then:

Q. 'What have you learned now?'

A. 'That it gets bigger when you come this way.'

Q. 'Do you mean that distance matters?'

A. 'Yes'.

Q. 'Which distance?'

A. 'This distance.' She ran her hand from the screen to the ring.

Q. 'Look! I am making a shadow with my hand. Now I am

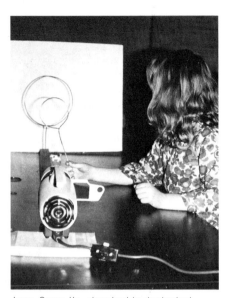

Jane, Stage IIa, absorbed in rhythmical growth of the shadow.

putting my other hand to touch it and I only get one shadow, don't I? But my hands are both the same size. Could you manage to get only one shadow with two rings, although they are different sizes?'

A. 'Yes!'

Jane then fixed the longest ring fairly near the screen and gradually drew a medium ring back all the way from the screen, past the fixed ring and still further back until the shadows coincided.

When she was asked if she could estimate where to put the other two rings to get coinciding shadows, she guessed wildly and then again found the position by trial.

When all four rings were fixed in position, she remarked that they were in sequence, but she did not notice that the distances from the light were halved each time although she had been encouraged to measure the diameters and to find that they were 20 centimetres, 10 centimetres, 5 centimetres and $2\frac{1}{2}$ centimetres respectively. In fact she was fascinated by the steady growth of the shadow as the rings were moved. This is, after all, proportion. But she could not focus on to this proportion when the positions became static.

In her own thinking Jane was at Stage II*a*, but she could easily understand an adult's reasoning up to Stage II*b*.

STAGE II*a*, VERY NEAR TO II*b*: A group of four children set about solving the problem as a team.

They were all quite sure of the fact that the sizes of the rings influence the sizes of the shadows and made no effort to demonstrate that influence. They stated, too, that position made a difference and volunteered to demonstrate that point.

Q. 'Which distance?'

A. 'The distance from the light,' said three of the four.

The fourth considered it was the distance from the screen but was soon overruled when the others reminded him that he 'ought to know'. We presumed that they had been told the fact and had believed it. None said that both distances could make a difference.

Then came the question, 'Could you make the shadow of a small ring exactly cover the shadow of a large one?'

They did this by trial and error, but it was interesting to note that, in their first effort, they tried to put one larger ring nearer the light and the smaller one on the screenward side of it.

Then one ring was put into position for them and the question was posed,

'Could you decide where to move it to to make its shadow twice as big as it is now?'

They went into action as an enthusiastic, well-knit team,

100

A group of juniors:
(a) first efforts, trial and error

(b) rings coming into sequence by trial and error

(c) realizing measurements might be useful.

measured the shadow and measured the distance from the screen. But they did not know what to do about that distance so they guessed a position and failed. They tried with a different ring, went through the same process and, of course, failed again. Over and over again they tried, every time measuring the distance of the ring from the screen and debating with one another what to do to that length. They tried adding on the diameter. They even tried adding on the length of the stalk. They did, in fact, try doubling the length. But not once, in fifteen minutes, did they measure the distance from the light.

This not only demonstrated Piaget's claims about the difficulty of searching for an inverse, as contrasted to a direct, proportion. It also showed very clearly that imposed teaching can indoctrinate but that it will not convince children of a scientific truth to the extent of concept formation.

STAGE II*b*: Robin was undoubtedly at Stage II*b* all the time that he was experimenting. One ring was put in place for him and he was asked, 'Could you place this second smaller ring so that it casts a shadow that will exactly cover the first shadow? Tell us what you are doing, and why.'

Robin was quite quiet for a whole minute as he moved the second ring along, first rapidly and then with very careful precision, until the shadows coincided. He fixed the stalk of the ring into position and said, 'There it is.'

Robin, Stage IIb, sure of how to make a shadow grow steadily. '

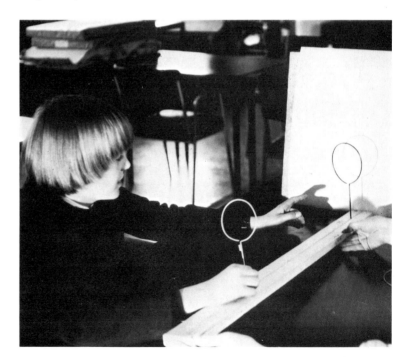

'How did you find the position? Will you do it again and explain?'

Robin: 'Well. It was a smaller ring than that one, so when they were very close together it cast a smaller shadow, so I moved it further back to make the shadow larger.'

'What do you mean by further back?'

Robin: 'From the screen', obviously showing that his preoccupation was still with the distance from the screen rather than from the light.

'Did you say that, with the ring further from the screen, the shadow gets bigger, or was it smaller?'

Robin: 'The further you take the ring back from the screen the shadow gets steadily bigger.'

Q. 'Could you think of another way of saying that?'

Robin: 'It grows.'

Later, as he watched Lesley and saw that she first went through the same movement and then cast a glance back at the light, he whispered to his neighbour, 'Oh! You could move the light.'

The word 'steadily' was perhaps the most revealing word that Robin spoke. It was clear that, intuitively, he saw rhythm in the growth but he had not yet thought clearly of that rhythm being mathematical proportion. Also he was conscious of distance from the light being of importance but inverse correspondence was more difficult for him to concentrate upon than the direct correspondence suggested by the distance from the screen.

STAGE IIIa: There was no doubt that Lesley, within a few seconds, showed herself to be at Stage IIIa. She ran the smaller ring backwards from the screen watching the shadow and, immediately the two shadows approximately coincided, she cast a quick glance back at the light. The glance was more telling than any words would have been. When given a third ring of intermediate size she explored only the region between the other two rings. As she did this she was still, obviously, at intervals, glancing at the length of board between the 'new' ring and the light. She was expecting the rings to form a cone shape from the light source yet she could not see it clearly enough to explain it except as 'light rays spreading out'. Her words were, in fact, few and far between. Her hypothetical thinking about the problem was intense and laborious as is to be expected at her age. She needed time to think and it would have been damaging to hurry her. She counted the holes from the light to each ring position but only estimated the difference of size of rings. Consequently sometimes, but not always, she could obtain a position immediately.

Lesley, Stage IIIa, conscious of the importance of distance from the light source.

Probably within a few weeks, this ability would have crystallized into the clear realization Permjit illustrates overleaf.

Permjit, Stage IIIb, calculating her third position between the rings.

STAGE IIIb: Permjit had very little difficulty in solving the problem of the shadows although, first of all, she did indeed seem to be attempting it by trial and error for she held the second ring near the screen, ran it back until the shadows coincided, and plugged it in. But then, in response to a question as to whether she could do it any other way, she took careful measurement of the two rings and of the distance of the light from the fixed ring, worked out her proportion sum and showed that the result gave the position of her second ring.

'Could you do it for a third ring?' she was asked.

'Yes! The same way!' she said. She repeated the arithmetical process and confidently fixed in the third ring.

All the above is perfect for Stage IIIb. The only puzzling feature was that she ignored as a measuring device the regularly spaced holes that were sunk all along the board between the light and the screen. Instead she had to use a foot ruler.

Concluding statement

The conclusions that can be drawn from the foregoing investigation are simple but vital.

The Stage II developments which build up to the true understanding of geometrical proportion last right through junior- and possibly all through secondary-school life. Nothing can be rushed at this stage. Equally, there can be no justifiable excuse for a teacher failing to help the concept mature. The wealth of experience that comes with the incessant handling of materials,

104

such as these shadow-casting rings, and the concrete reasoning that results, are an essential build-up for a true understanding of the geometry that will be learned when the period of formal thinking is reached. The pattern of thinking that involves inverse proportion is very slow and late in maturing.

Unlike most chapters, this one has dealt with a theme that appears explicitly in many of Piaget's books instead of in just one (or two) of them. Cross-referencing of this sort offers the richest and most rewarding way of studying the Piagetian view of developmental psychology. It is interesting to compare this study of a child's development of an understanding of geometrical proportion not only with the study of proportionate reasoning described in Chapter Ten, but also with the Piagetian theme of the development of a sense of proportion in moral and ethical matters as described in Piaget's *The Moral Judgment of the Child*.

CHAPTER TWELVE

The mental lattice — full hypothetical reasoning
(Testing children's propositional logic through the mixing of colourless chemicals)

This was probably the most searching test from Piaget's *Growth of Logical Thinking*[1] that we repeated with children at Chorley. Each child who asked to 'do the puzzle' was given four bottles of colourless, odourless liquids: these were perceptually identical except for being marked No. 1, No. 2, No. 3, No. 4. The child was also given a differently shaped bottle marked X and a supply of empty jars.

The tester knew that the bottles contained the following chemicals:[2] No. 1 Dilute hydrogen peroxide solution. No. 2 Water. No. 3 Ferrous ammonium sulphate solution. No. 4 EDTA solution (ethylene diamine tetra-acetic acid disodium salt). X Potassium thiocyanate solution (the colorant). He also knew that ferrous ammonium sulphate is further oxidized, to ferric ammonium sulphate, by the addition of hydrogen peroxide and that the colorant will redden this. EDTA decolorizes it. Water is only a dilutant, having no effect on the colour.

The experimenter had previously put a little of 1+3 into a jar (J) and he let the child watch a drop of X turn the liquid red. He told the child that the liquid in J had come from one or more of the bottles, 1, 2, 3, 4, and asked him to discover which one, or which ones, it had come from. Children were allowed to experiment either solo or in small groups. In the latter case their arguments with one another were recorded and these were, at times, more revealing of their true thinking than answers to adult questions might have been.

It will be seen that the whole solution to this problem can only be reached through the experimenter forming, mentally, a clear plan of action, or 'combinatorial system',[3] in which every possible combination of the liquids in the first four bottles is tested, in turn, with X. In other words, he must form a mental

[1] Chapter 7.
[2] Piaget used: 1 Sulphuric acid. 2 Water. 3 Oxygenated water. 4 Thiosulphate. 5 Potassium iodide, but we found the other chemicals easier to use.
[3] Jean Piaget & Bärbel Inhelder, *The Growth of Logical Thinking*, p. 107.

'lattice' of all possible links of 1, 2, 3 and 4, e.g. (a) 1, (b) 2, (c) 3, (d) 4, (e) 1+2, (f) 1+3, (g) 1+4, (h) 2+3, (i) 2+4, (j) 3+4, (k) 1+2+3, etc., etc., and then he must put forward the proposition:

'One or more of these possible combinations is what I am searching for,' and then, fifteen times over, he must hypothesize: 'If it is (a) . . .' (or 'If it is (b) . . .', etc.), then X will turn (a) red, and if X does not turn (a) red, then (a) is not the combination I am looking for.'

Only then, having set out mentally his structured programme of action, does he experiment.

Only at this final intellectual stage (Stage IIIb) can this mental operation be carried out, since it is not until then that what Piaget calls the necessary 'operational schema' can develop in the child in a general form. The stage is generally reached in mid-teenage though it is seen in a raw form (Stage IIIa) somewhat earlier. The stages that are passed through in reaching this climax are as follows:

STAGE I: The child mixes the liquids quite at random, sometimes by chance producing the colour. His explanations of his results are anything but logical.

STAGE IIa: The child, on entering what, in general, Piaget calls the 'period of concrete operations', is systematic enough to make sure that he adds X to every one of the liquids 1—4 though not necessarily in an understandable sequence. Only with strong encouragement from adults does he mix two or more of the liquids before adding X (except possibly pouring together all four plus X) and then, once adult encouragement is withdrawn, he returns to adding X to the single liquids only. He seems to consider that the colour is *in* one of the liquids and that it can be made to show and then be hidden again. His only suggestions as to why colour does not result are that there is too much or too little 'water' (i.e. colourless liquid) or that it is something to do with the sequence of mixing. Never does he consider the necessary exclusion of No. 4 — nor does he consider that the colour comes from the combination of several liquids rather than existing in just one of them.

STAGE IIb: At this stage the child spontaneously tries combinations of the two, three or all four liquids with X but he does not find any systematic way of doing so. His combinations are empirical and tentative. But whatever combinations he tries, the child still considers the colour to be brought forth from one of the liquids rather than through the act of combining several of them.

STAGE IIIa: Three innovations appear at this level and it is only the perfecting of them that makes Stage IIIb any different from IIIa. The three innovations are: (a) the child begins to use a

107

systematic method of working out the possible combinations of the four liquids. This is partly demonstrated by a decision to record in writing what linkings he has tried. (*b*) The child begins to show signs of forming the concept of the possibility of a complete fusion of liquids from several of the bottles producing an entirely new substance that is coloured. (*c*) Having found a solution in 1+3+X, he does not leave the experiment as completed but continues to explore in case there are further combinations that will produce the colour. (This is, of course, an extension of (*a*).)

The combination of these three innovations shows, in the child's intellectual approach, a move towards a general logical structure of deductive reasoning involving conjunction, implication, incompatibility, exclusion and so forth, that is, in itself, a lattice of mental actions which dovetails with the lattice of possible chemical mixtures already mentioned.

The distinction between incompatibility (i.e. that No. 4 is incompatible, since it decolorizes the red liquid) and exclusion (i.e. No. 2 can be excluded as an agent in the colouring process since the resultant liquid, after it has been added, can be either clear or red), is not obvious to the child at Stage III*a*: it is obvious to the child at Stage III*b*.

The following photographs were taken, and interviews or conversations were recorded, when a group of children of all ages chose to do this 'puzzle' from among many that were available to them.

STAGES I, II*a* and II*b*: The children photographed here were all quite unable to give a reasoned solution to the problem yet all were keen to produce the pretty colour in the liquids. They all still assumed that the colour would be brought out of one of the liquids by the action of another. Before reaching the stage of formal reasoning they could not envisage it as being due to combination as such, for combination is, in itself, an abstraction. These three children were not tested separately but were observed as they played and argued together, and their conversation was recorded.

Christopher (Stage II*a*) was the leading member of the group. He was convinced that X would 'bring the colour out' from one of the other liquids and he tried it with 1, with 2, with 3, and with 4, but in random order, sometimes by chance trying the same one a second time. Marjorie (II*b*) suggested mixing several of the liquids at the same time with X and did so herself, also in random order. Christopher was led by her into doing the same. Nicola Claire (Stage I) watched in awe, occasionally pushing forward a bottle and saying, 'Try this.'

108

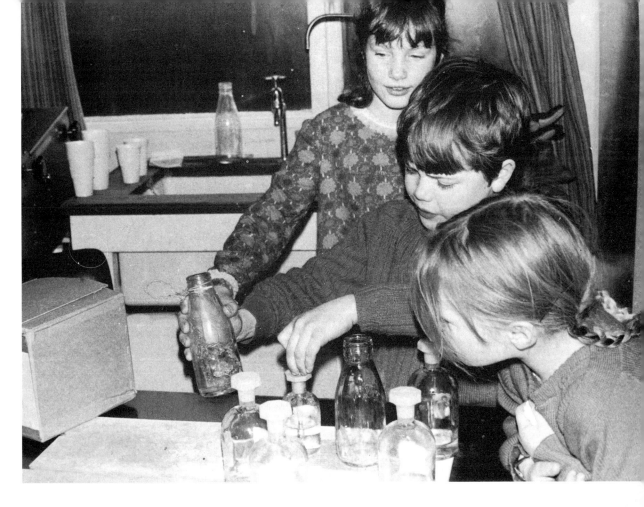

When, by chance, the colour was achieved each child was quite satisfied that he or she personally had solved the whole problem.

STAGE IIIa: It was obvious that Nicola Ann had formed a mental plan of action before she started to mix the chemicals. She seemed to need to support this mental plan physically by her first obvious action. This was to set out the bottles 1 to 4 in a neat row, very evenly spaced. In front of them she placed X.

Systematically she tested each separate chemical with X and then, equally systematically, she started on the combinations of two chemicals with X. Soon $(1+3)+X$ was reached and Nicola was rewarded with the reddening of the liquid. For a moment she was satisfied that she had solved the whole problem: then, perhaps, our silence as we watched her focused her thoughts on to further possibilities.

She said, 'There might be a second answer, mightn't there? Now, where was I?'

A group (Stages I, IIa, IIb) exploring together.

109

Nicola Ann, Stage IIIa, is very methodical.

With her eyes on the bottles she counted on her fingers, 'I've done 1 with 2, and 1 with 3. Now it's 1 with 4.'

After testing $(1+4)+X$, she queried aloud whether she could do more and, at this point, started jotting down notes. This resulted in her testing $(2+3)+X$ and $(2+4)+X$.

After another pensive moment she said, 'Now, I must do 3 plus the others.'

To our amusement she started with $(3+1)+X$ and, for a second or so, was delighted to see the colour emerge. Then, as she wrote it down, she exclaimed, 'Oh! It's the same as $1+3$. Then I don't need $3+2$ either.' She tried $(3+4)+X$ and accepted the result calmly.

From this point on Nicola Ann was completely systematic. When colour was created by $(1+2+3)+X$ she was puzzled for a moment; then she consulted her notes and remarked, 'It doesn't seem to matter whether 2 is there or not.'

She eliminated $(1+2+4)$ quite normally and then said, '$1+3$ will do it anyway, won't it? But I suppose I had better try it with 4.' As she added 4 and watched the colour disappear her only

110

remark was, 'Oh!' and then, 'Now I'd better put them all together, I suppose.'

We interrupted her and asked her what she would expect to be the result of doing so. Her forecast was correct though laboriously produced. Then came a few more crucial questions and answers:

'What do you think really produced the colour?' we asked.

'It was 3', she said; then, as we were silent 'Well! 1 with 3.'

'Was the colour in one of them?'

'No! It was sort of made by them both.'

'How?'

'I suppose a chemical reaction made something new and red.'

'Then how did 4 eliminate the red?'

'I don't know. That's the bit that is really puzzling.'

Nicola continued to puzzle for some time and then moved on to other interests. We decided it was best to leave her to return to this final part of the problem whenever she felt motivated to do so for only then would she be likely to solve it.

STAGE IIIb: Dorothy, experimenting some time later, and having considered Nicola Ann's results, solved the problem completely.

Dorothy, Stage IIIb, works confidently through her lattice.

Concluding statement

This experiment illustrates particularly the subtle way in which the alert adult mind organizes an overall structure (or 'mental-lattice') of all the possible combinations of factors that need to be tested when one is searching for the solution to a problem. Each such combination then needs to be put to the test by some mental 'group' activity as the INRC activity or operational schema.

For truly formal reasoning, both the lattice activity and the group activity must be *mentally* conclusive. This can be illustrated by examples from geometrical proofs. In this example, with chemicals, the lattice was mentally achieved but the group activity, while mentally planned, was concluded through practical demonstration. As contrasted to the example in Chapter Eight, this example does not demand the application of the principle of 'all other things being equal' since here it is combinations that are being looked for and not isolations.

This is also just a further strong example of the change in intellectual activity that takes place in most people in early adolescence. Empirical practical searching for a solution, followed by a verbal and mental explanation of results, is reversed. Now it becomes a hypothetical planning of possible results, followed by mental reasoning or by practical demonstrations that ensue from this mental plan.

WHERE DOES IT ALL LEAD US?

Let me become personal. Where does it lead me?

It leads me to realize that, in every matter, every day, every child will have a point of view different from my own. And, to him his point of view will be the interesting one, the precious one and, if he is very young, the only one. I still have the advantage, of course. For, given patience and perceptiveness, I can understand his point of view as well as mine while he does not even know that mine exists.

For a toddler, his standpoint will be quite egocentric. For a young infant it will be intuitive and preconceptual. The junior will find interest in the fact that I can offer a different approach to a problem: he will even be convinced that he understands my approach while, in fact, he is only conscious of the practically applicable part of it. The mentally satisfying experience of holding a whole pattern of innumerable solutions concurrently in one's consciousness, to meditate and work upon them, has not yet touched him.

Few would doubt that this viewpoint, or this skill of hypothetical reasoning, is the richer and more mature one. It has been nurtured by the experiences of one's lifetime and fed on the cumulative learning of the generations of peoples in the cultures in which one has lived. Every child has a right to be helped towards this rich inheritance. But at any moment in time he can only take a step towards it from where he stands at that moment — from his point of view, at his stage of intellectual growth.

Whoever I am, whatever my relationship to him may be, I owe it to him to seek to understand his point of view so that I may diagnose his needs. Then I can wisely enrich the environment in which he will enjoy learning and developing intellectual skills. He will learn plentifully from his environment without any help from me, for he learns from everything that he experiences or that he does. But he will learn the more richly if I, who am a part of his environment, help him forward in this scientific way. He must be, as Nathan Isaacs said, 'architect of his own growth'. I owe it to him to perceive his needs and to supply him with the right materials with which to build happily and without strain.

The preceding chapters have shown something, in a simplified way, of what Piaget has diagnosed as being a child's way of thinking at different stages of his intellectual development. But here it is very simplified. Those who want to know more can enjoy reading it in the wealth of books that Piaget has written himself. How we adapt this understanding to our own ways of helping children learn is a challenge to parents and teachers alike. A few explorations into precipitating such learning are described in the appendices that follow.

APPENDIX I

'Megalithic mathematics' in the primary school

PART I

This is an account of a project carried out by a team of six students (with their tutor and class teacher) in which a class of thirty-six junior children were given scope to exercise their developing skill of 'concrete reasoning'[1] and encouragement in forming the concepts of weight, of volume and of scale.[2] As the children saw it, the whole object of the exercise was to measure up Stonehenge[3] and make a model of it. As the students and staff saw it, the object was to precipitate a learning situation based on Piagetian theory.

Preparation of materials

The students had visited Stonehenge in advance, numbered the stones, made six catalogue cards (on to which measurements and calculations were to be entered against each stone's number) and made a sketch-map of the site. This was divided into six sections, one for each team of six children.

The students made a preparatory visit to the school, discussed with the children what they hoped to do and introduced the catalogue cards to them. They supervised the preparation of cardboard clinometers, yardsticks (showing feet and yards only), skipping-ropes joined together and knotted at fathom intervals, and any other measuring devices that children suggested. One child, Muriel, came to college of her own accord and practised using her clinometer by measuring the height of a church spire. She was accurate (by luck!) within 4 feet. Her skill and enthusiasm made her as useful as an extra student on the field-work day.

Field work at Stonehenge

The students went out to Stonehenge in advance of the children and fixed the catalogue number of each stone to the ground

A catalogue card.

[1] See Chapter One, pp. 12–15, on stages of intellectual development.
[2] See Chapter One, pp. 14–15, on concepts that develop at a stage later than infancy.
[3] The full permission of the Ministry of Works was obtained in advance.

Measuring with a tape measure.
Measuring with six-foot sticks.

with a skewer. We should have liked the children to do this but we were facing a shortage of time as they had only two hours there.

From the moment they arrived, the children worked with real enthusiasm and remained engrossed in the work until the very end. Each group was given its catalogue card and the rough sketch-map of the stones which, and between which, they were to measure. One student supervised each group of six children. They measured every stone by at least two methods, one being geometrical. If a discrepancy in the pairs of measurements was at all great children rejected them and started again; if it was small they took an average or estimated which to accept by comparing the stone with other stones. They often insisted on measuring the girth, with tape-measures, to check the thickness and breadth. Each measurement, as it was obtained, was catalogued in the appropriate space on a card. Further spaces on the cards were completed in later weeks.

Their favourite geometrical method of measuring was by holding a pencil at arm's length, sighting a stone, running a thumb down the pencil until the height of the stone was exactly matched by the pencil length above the thumb-nail, turning the pencil through a right angle so that it was horizontal, then sending another child to mark the horizontal line thus acquired: this was then measured. The children were utterly fascinated that a measurement could be taken indirectly. A favourite method with the boys was hurling a skipping-rope over the lintels and counting the knots. The difficult task of getting the rope over impressed the children with the massiveness of the stones. Other

116

visitors to the site, British and American, soon joined in by jumping for dangling ropes or by hoisting children up to reach them.

Miriam and a partner, using a clinometer, measured the angle subtended by each large stone in their section at the end of a measured base line, and reproduced it on squared paper to get the height of each stone. They demonstrated their skill to the other groups and several other children consequently tried out this method. Their other varied ways of measuring can be seen in the photographs.

Before leaving Stonehenge, the children completed the measurements of the ground plan too. And they were allowed to collect small specimens of the stone for weighing. We checked for pieces that were about a cubic inch in size and the keeper ascertained that, geologically, they were the same as the trilithons.

Indirectly measuring a height with a clinometer.

A clinometer.

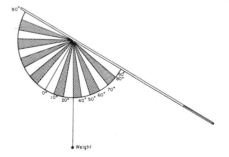

Measuring with knotted skipping ropes.

Calculating from entries on the catalogue card.

Starting a scale model

In our next session at the school we achieved two things. Each group started modelling its own stones to a scale of 1 inch to 4 feet. The word 'scale' was not used at first. The clay was shaped directly on to $\frac{1}{4}$-inch graph paper, covering one side of a square with clay for each foot of stone. As the students saw the children becoming quite adept at this system they asked:

'Do you realize you are working to scale?'

Most of the children had not realized this at all, but a few of them were beginning to get a vague feeling of appreciation of it. This vague feeling represented a very early stage in the development of the concept of geometrical proportion.[4]

The other thing that some children did that week was to weigh the pieces of stone and find their cubic capacity. To do this they had to know what cubic measurement was. The students

[4] See Chapter Eleven, p. 97.

Modelling to scale.

Using the overflow can.

dealt with this problem by modelling inch cubes of clay and asking the children in their groups to guess their size. They obtained the usual answers of 'an inch' or 'an inch each way' and so on. Eventually, they introduced the terms 'sugar cubes' and 'Oxo cubes' and ultimately 'inch cubes'. The children were then asked to make an inch-cube hole in a lump of clay and fill it with water. They answered readily when asked how much water the hole held but, when it was poured from the hole into a tin lid, there was some argument before they realized that the amount of water remained a cubic inch. This, again, represented an early stage of a development of a concept.[5]

With a few children the students managed to encourage further progress towards a concept of volume by introducing an overflow can. Children filled it until it just overflowed from the spout. Then they tried pouring in a further cubic inch of water

[5] Volume is a late-developing concept, although the concept of quantity develops early.

and measuring what came out. Interesting arguments arose as to whether it was the same water that came out. We encouraged this debate, for we saw it as another exercise in concrete reasoning. Then they dropped in a cubic inch of clay and found that a cubic inch of water overflowed. And they followed up this idea by dropping in bits of Stonehenge stone until one such piece displaced a cubic inch of water. Two of the children fully understood that this was therefore a cubic inch of stone and they tried, with some success, to persuade other children of the fact. They made a careful note of the weight of 'a cubic inch of Stonehenge'.

Discovering a cubic foot
The next week the students pressed the understanding of cubic measurement a bit further by organizing the 'manufacture' of a cubic foot. They asked the whole class to model inch cubes of clay and asked them to pack them neatly into the space made by four rulers fixed together to form a square hollow.

It was interesting to see the empirical way in which a few children soon devised a form of mass production. One little clique pressed long 'snakes' of clay between four rulers and then removed the rulers and chopped off inches from the resulting solid. It was also interesting to notice how some children remonstrated immediately any one of their peers put his cube in untidily. To us all this was painfully slow, but sure, concrete reasoning.

They formed the idea of twelve rows of twelve cubes long before the last row was complete. In fact, quite early on they were putting in rows in both directions.

When the first layer was complete some were sure that they now had a cubic foot; and they thought, too, that 144 cubic inches were 'an awful lot' considering what a long time they took to make. They were too disheartened for us to be happy about it when we produced a carboard foot cube and they realized that twelve such layers of inch cubes would be needed before they could finish the job. They soon revived and worked out that this would mean a need for 1,728 cubic inches.[6] They accepted the figure placidly. It meant nothing to them for it was too big to be meaningful. A few boys carried on for a time trying to complete a cubic foot but soon gave up in despair. Even this despair was just one small step further towards what we were now appreciating as a concept of cubic capacity developing in the children.

A few, laboriously and with the help of a book of tables, multiplied up 1,728 times the weight of a cubic inch and found the weight of a cubic foot of stone but this was, in fact, an illustration of how junior children do not learn through the

---

[6] i.e., twelve layers of 144 inch cubes.

practice of rote methods. While they were proud of their results and while a few remembered the resultant weight a week later, it was all too obvious that none of this last part of the work had truly been digested.

Completing the stones to scale
On our fourth afternoon, again at the school, we finished off modelling the stones to scale. There was not much left to be done. Then some of the class spent much of the time in calculating and entering on the charts the weights of actual stones. And they weighed and measured (and recorded) the modelled stones that had dried out from the previous week. We found that some children had taken home the measurements of the stones in their sector of Stonehenge and worked out their volumes and weights for the charts. Some had really formed concepts but others had merely worked mechanically.

Mathematics of a kiln
In order to fire the model stones we had to build a primitive kiln. The students had taken some miniature bricks ($\frac{1}{2}$ inch long) to school and shown the children how the kiln could be built. They sent a team, made up of one child from each group, to measure bricks on the corner of the school wall and to calculate how many bricks the class must bring to build a kiln 2 feet high and of the square measurement that would just be covered by a dust-bin lid. These amounted to about eighty. The average number each child would have to bring was worked out. We prepared a large sheet of graph paper with 'Bricks' marked on the vertical axis and allowing for children's names below the horizontal axis. The intention was to stick on the graph paper a bright 1-inch square of coloured paper for each brick brought and see whose was the tallest column. The children were excited about this, since it was their first block graph, but it was brought to an untimely end when one girl arrived at school escorted by her father who was wheeling a whole barrow-load of bricks.

The fifth week was an exciting one when we built and fired the kiln. Each group in turn laid a course of bricks, packed it with sawdust and embedded its stones in it. The children had to give intensive thought to the simple laying of a square base and each group, after the first, had the puzzle of laying their course so as to interlock with the course below. It was interesting to see how each group, as it finished its course, looked in satisfaction at the overlapping and seemed to get an aesthetic thrill from the geometry of it. The children were also keen to explain afterwards how the bricks had locked together.

The kiln.

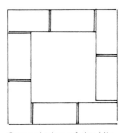
Ground plan of the kiln.

121

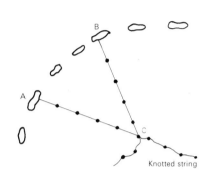

Plotting an interior position with knotted string triangles.

Preparing the ground plan

As most of the class got down to the task of weighing and measuring their fired stones, painting them grey, estimating losses of weight and shrinkages and recording their results on the charts, a group of children started the ground plan for the completed model. The scale was, of course, the same as for the stones – 1 inch to 4 feet. The children soon discovered that we needed a circle of 32 inches diameter but, to our surprise, they had difficulty in seeing that half that figure, 16 inches, was needed for the radius. They were shown how to use a length of looped string as a radius and had great difficulty in describing their first circle. They did not think of reducing it by one-tenth to correspond with the stones' shrinkage and we decided it would be unwise to point it out, as a solution of the problem would necessitate abstract reasoning on their part.

They filled this circle with a wet mixture of sand and 'Polyfilla' as a base to hold the stones. But before doing this, each group marked the positions of its stones on a similar circle of paper (divided into sections) so that positions could be pricked through on to the base. It was done this way because the children worked more slowly than the mixture dried out.

Siting the stones

Each group fixed the positions of its stones by simple measurement to scale round the outside circle and by triangulation from two such stones to find the positions of the ones in the interior.

They constructed the triangles, working in threes, by using string knotted at 1-inch intervals. One child held an end of the string on each of the two circumference stones while another counted the inches needed on each string and held them so that they met; then the third marked the apex so constructed. The argument and discussion that ensued during this exercise was of very real value to the children in nurturing their 'concrete reasoning'. In this way all the stones were at last sited and erected, according to their catalogue numbers, to complete the scale model of Stonehenge.

Conclusions

From a Piagetian point of view we considered we had evidence that, for the children, this work provided experience towards the formation of the late-developing concepts of weight and volume, cubic capacity, proportion and scale. It gave early pre-geometrical experience in angles and in the construction of a triangle with three given sides and in the meaning of the radius of a circle. The simple experience with sketch-maps may have been too forced: if we were repeating this project it would be wise to precede it by the diagnostic test on co-ordinates described in Chapter Three. It would be wise, too, to give further experience of work with angles by working on shadows and the angle of the sun at the solstice. The greatest real value of the work to children was the concrete reasoning involved all the way through, for this is the period of their lives in which most children are exercising their fast-developing reasoning powers by using their concepts, together with concrete materials, to solve problems empirically and then to demonstrate their findings.

One could list further Piagetian examples if there were also space here to describe the intensive writing and the art that arose naturally from the project. Instead it might be a better use of space to give a quick account, mostly in photographic form, of the children's own exploration about the probable mechanics of transporting and lifting the stones.

PART II 'Operation Heave Ho!'

The children paid a second visit to Stonehenge but, this time, without such a specific plan of action as on the first occasion. They gazed in awe at the stones, now seeing them with even greater respect since they had made their model. They gazed into the distance across Salisbury Plain and discussed the long haul over which the stones had had to be moved (and they were probably unable to envisage this journey as being from beyond the horizon). They measured the circumference of the circle with a 'click wheel', home-made from an old bicycle wheel, that had a marmalade tin lid to make the clicks. At the tutor's suggestion they divided and found out that there were 'three and a bit' times as many clicks round the circumference as across the diameter. Another group of boys took the same measurements with what they called the 'giant strider' — an enormous pair of wooden dividers, 4 feet tall and fixed open at a permanent angle. Of course the two groups compared answers. They did the same with the circle of 'Aubrey Holes' and with the circular ditch, each time dividing and finding the answer of 'three and a bit' but 'not always the same size bits'.

'When are the bits big and when are they small?' they asked. What bliss ignorance of inaccuracy can be!

Back at school, next day, they compared and graphically recorded circumferences and diameters of other circular things and a few of them began to see a generalization in the answers.

While we were still at Stonehenge the biggest surprise came to the adults of the party when two boys expressed dissatisfaction at having found the girth of the stones only at their base.

'Look Sir! They are narrower at the top,' they said.

We taught them the word 'taper' and asked, 'Well! Can you do anything about it at that height?'

'No! It's too high to climb up.' And they mooched off.

Minutes later they returned.

'Will you hold these two yardsticks for us,' they asked, 'so that we can measure the angle of taper?'

With two yardsticks and the protractor from their home-made clinometer, they found the angle to be 13 degrees; then they drew the stone to scale and cut off 13 degrees from each side. Fired with success, they measured the 'angle of taper' of the other stones and found a general tapering of 13 degrees which was something none of us had known about.

The click-wheel.

125

The dramatic work was done on the site at Stonehenge but it was back in their small, crowded classroom and playground that more exciting results were achieved.

Mechanics Stage I — in the field

We had told them, before they went to Stonehenge, that the chief problems we hoped they would solve were how the stones could have been transported and raised. Simultaneously the headmaster had put a see-saw in the school playground. As with the 'click wheel', it was a primitive one; it was merely a steel ladder across two gymnasium forms. Children from all the classes piled on it at playtimes, lengthening and shortening the distance from the fulcrum to each end according to the unequal weight of children on either end. After some days the headmaster and his assistant approached and asked for a turn. And they both climbed on to the same end.

The children knew them well enough to suspect a mathematical problem at once, and solved it correspondingly quickly by rationing the length of ladder the two heavy men could have to sit on. So two small children on the longer end triumphantly raised the masters into the air. We saw this as a very early stage of intuitive realization of what leverage is all about.

The see-saw.

After play, in the 'top' classroom, they chatted about levers and fulcrums for a time and tested out, by feeling only, the pressure from their own fingers when levering up weights of various suitable objects that had been left on the bench. They tried levering off tin lids, too, with halfpennies,[7] pennies and with gradually increasing lengths, until they levered off one most easily of all with a long-handled screwdriver. At no time, to this point, was Stonehenge or its stones mentioned.

Mechanics Stage II – exploration for figures

A few days later we dumped in the school garden the only suitable heavy objects we could acquire and we called them Stonehenge stones. They were an oblong lump of concrete, a heavy steel plank and a paving stone. We challenged the children to transport them to a suitable spot and erect them, using no more of their own strength at any one time than gentle hand pressure and only fine string if they wanted pulleys.

One group decided that the spot where its stone was lying was 'suitable' and they started digging a hole at its end immediately. But they made the mistake of digging it exactly at its end and so left themselves a slight transport problem. The others dug their hole some distance away and were faced with a major transport problem. For a whole double period and for a good many

7 Old coinage.

Four attempts at lifting the stones.

playtimes on future days they worked at their task, fetching one of us to see every development that interested them. We were rather pleased at their own critical powers in deciding what developments and discoveries were important enough to show us. As usual we encouraged their discussion and argument and 'concrete reasoning'.

It was towards the end of the first morning that one of them ejaculated, 'Look, Sir! It's just like a see-saw.'

The first group had erected its stone before the second had transported it to the hole. After numerous trials and errors they

had levered and wedged the end up, a bit at a time, and jammed soil underneath until it was at about an angle of 60 degrees from the horizontal, at which stage it had slipped, still slanting, into the hole. The ingenuity with which they tried to get extra pressure, by using rulers with weights on the end as levers, can be seen in some of the pictures. And they used wedges and props, once they had realized the see-saw analogy, to try to get the 'fulcrum' nearer the high end. They raised it the final 30° to the vertical by more wedging and by pulling on fine string tied to the top. We had hoped that they would think of a winch

Measuring the drag of the stone on rollers.

at this stage but the idea did not come. Meanwhile the other team had solved its transport problem by laying a roadway of fine soil, stamped hard, and rolling the 'stone' along on pencils.

Mechanics Stage III — laboratory conditions
We thought that the rough ideas about method had now settled into their thoughts and that the time had come for accurate measuring.

Back in the classroom we asked them to make a very heavy, small parcel of suitable shape, so they filled a rectangular box with heavy oddments. It weighed 50 ounces. We showed them how to fit a spring balance to a gap in the string and how to register the pull needed for various dragging or lifting operations. They dragged this 'stone' across desks and tables, across the playground, up a ramp in the playground and up various artificial ramps in the classroom measuring and recording results all the time. They did the same tests with the stone on rollers and some of the tests with the stone on a raft in the school garden pool. They discussed the different readings.

Very soon, as we expected, most children started recording the readings on block graphs. They recorded everything they could think of — facts that we, as adults, saw to be useful and others that we thought useless. Briefly these facts fell into two categories. First they recorded the pulls needed to draw the 'stone' along, at a reasonable, steady rate, over various surfaces, to pull it along on a raft, to pull it along on rollers and to pull it up slopes of various angles with and without rollers. (They used a long plank, a spirit-level and a home-made protractor for the angles.)

130

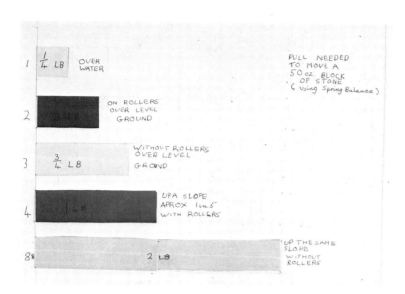

Graphs of recorded drag.

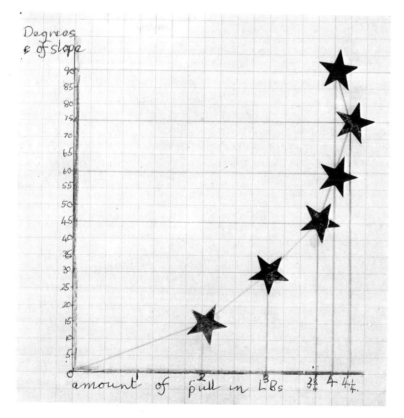

Secondly they recorded the lifting pull needed at different angles to lift the stone on to its own end.

It was this last effort that gave us teachers the greatest delight of all; a boy more or less stumbled on to the technique of polar-graphing. His genuine first attempt is reproduced opposite. Certainly, it has mistakes in it, according to our conventions — not only the 'kink' at 40 degrees. But we thought it hardly fair to criticize, on detail, an eleven-year-old who had produced on plain paper a technique that we, with the luxury of polar-graph paper, had had to be taught in our sixth forms. So the headmaster gave him some polar-graphing paper and he had the aesthetic thrill of reproducing his effort on that. It is difficult to say whether the final shape shows primarily the lift needed (at various angles) at the top or the weight supported at the bottom by the ground. A purist would say the graph was useless. But in so far as it shows the sum total of the two forces it is interesting. But, needless to say, he had not understood polar-graphing through stumbling on this one example of it. He had not generalized nor formulated a law.

The graphs mentioned so far were all drawn on paper. At our suggestion the children tried one interesting, solid representation of a graph. Over and over again they let the 'stone' fall gently from different angles on to a match-stick pressed lightly into plasticine to see how much further it would be thrust in by the impact. The result is too minute to be reproduced here but it taught us roughly how much damage a falling Stonehenge stone can do!

But it was the reverse of this that we had asked them to discover; and they discovered it. They knew now the pull needed to transport 50 ounces along horizontally: (a) on a raft, (b) on rollers.

They worked out the weights of various stones at Stonehenge (as in the earlier pages of this chapter) and found the pull needed to transport them on catamarans on Wiltshire rivers and on rollers on the flat part of Salisbury Plain. Then they measured and averaged the weights their headmaster and staff could pull. So they went on to find out how many men were needed to transport and then to raise a Stonehenge stone. Let us hope that Megalithic men were as strong as present-day headmasters! Overleaf is one child's estimate of the strength of Alderbury staff.

Finally, even when strong men like headmasters are skilful, ropes can break and so transportation can fail. Are ropes that are twisted together stronger than the total of the same number of strands of rope used separately?

The children set out to discover this with the following results: To represent rope they used strands of wool. First they tied

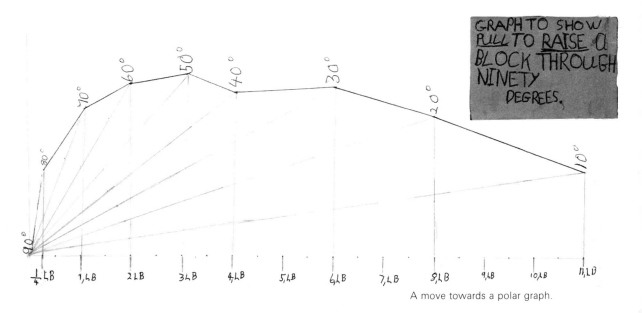

A move towards a polar graph.

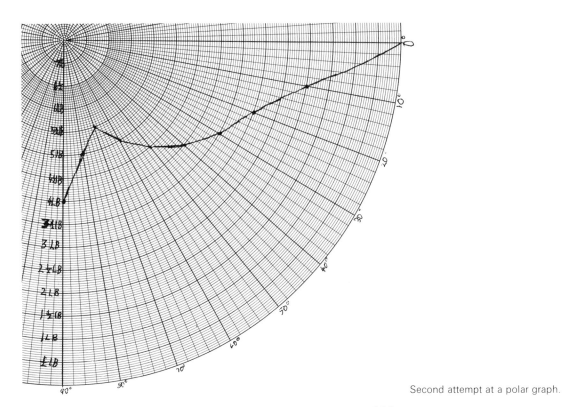

Second attempt at a polar graph.

How many men were need to
pull a stone at stonehenge?

We found that Mr Murray pulled
2 cwts. and Mr Norcliffe pulled 2½ cwts and
Mr Marsh pulled 1½ cwts. so the average
pull is

$$(2 \text{ cwts} + 2\tfrac{1}{2} \text{ cwts} + 1\tfrac{1}{2} \text{ cwts}) \div 3 = 2 \text{ cwts}.$$

Using 2 cwts as the average pull of a man and
if an average stone of stonehenge weighs 20 tons
which equals 400 cwts then by devideing 400 by 2
we find that 200 men are needed to pull a stone
along level ground without rollers. Using our
graph of previous experiments we see that we
need ⅓ of the pull needed along level ground
without rollers to pull along water. That
is ⅓ of 200 which is 66 approx. We should need
2 × 66 to pull along level ground with
rollers (132 men). When we pull the stone
up a slope with rollers we need 4 × 66 (264
men) Without rollers we need 8 × 66 or
528 men.

Nicola Pooley
age 10¾ yrs.

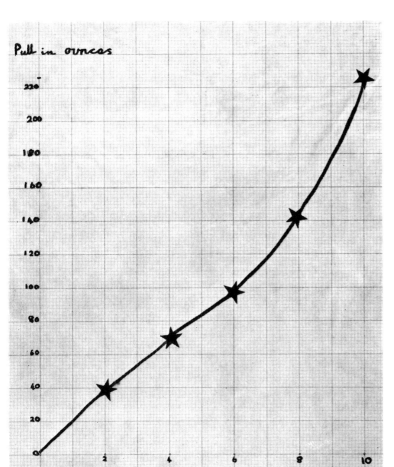

Pull in ounces

Number of strands.

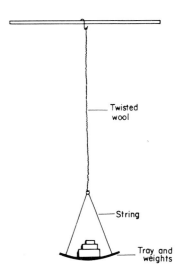

Twisted wool

String

Tray and weights

one strand, of a given length, to the hook of a spring balance and suspended a pan at the other end. On the pan they placed weights until they recorded the breaking-point of one strand of wool. They repeated this test with two strands of the same length, twisted together, and recorded the breaking-point again. Similarly, they recorded the breaking-point of four and of eight twisted strands and so forth.

Our final decision from the Stonehenge project was that even Megalithic men knew that unity is strength. But little did Megalithic men suspect, when they built their computer centuries ago, that they were preparing enjoyable lessons in junior mathematics and mechanics for children of today. Like mathematics itself, Stonehenge preserves its perfections and mysteries across the centuries, while still releasing them generously to those who request it.

Page 134:
An estimate of strength (letter).

135

APPENDIX II

Integrated learning through the building of a
Wendy House

This is a further example of integrated learning at the Concrete
Operational Stage of junior-school life that was carried out by a
class of 36 nine-year-old children and a group of training college
students. The whole project was inspired by the existence of a
strong wooden box (about 5 feet $\times$ 3$\frac{1}{2}$ feet $\times$ 2$\frac{1}{2}$ feet) that was, to
use a hackneyed phrase, 'too good to be wasted'.

The children asked for help in making the box into a 'Wendy
House' to give to a local children's home.

'Yes!' said the students, 'we will help you. But, if we do, will
you make a thorough job of it? Will you make a house that has
a hot-water system, an electricity system, well-tiled floors and so
forth? We will bring you equipment from which you can learn
how to do these things.'

The children agreed and formed themselves into gangs of work-
men. There were carpenters and plumbers, there were electricians
and tilers, plasterers and interior designers. Each gang agreed to
concentrate on its own task until the work was finished although,
at intervals, every child rested from his task and learned, considerably, by gazing at what others were doing. Students
supplied the children with learning materials, such as can be
seen in the pictures, and left the children to learn their trades by
exploring scientific principles through experiments with these
challenging materials and by discussing their results. Books
were available, too, and students were always at hand to
encourage the children with pertinent questions and occasional
suggestions.

Carpenters learned to use geometrical tools to get such properties as right angles and parallel sides before laboriously
sawing the house front, the false floor, the dividing wall be-

Transformation geometry through a tiling pattern.

tween the two rooms, the holes for windows and for the door. Lino-tilers showed fascination in working out a repeating pattern of hexagons for the floor of one room and of triangles for the other and held many incidental conversations with the students as to why unexpected cross-patterns evolved. In discussing the angles and sides in these patterns they were laying a foundation for later 'transformation geometry'. Artists potato-printed curtain material and 'string stamped' rolls of wallpaper.

Electricians soon discovered how to rig up a simple lighting circuit but they then spent a considerable time playing with the solenoid (a nail, dangling on string, that could be sucked into a coiled wire by a small electric current) on a toy railway signal. As a result of this learning, one boy ultimately made a stronger solenoid, worked by a 6-volt battery, that would open a lifting garage door made of polystyrene.

Plumbers, after two afternoons at work, had an experimental circulation of water rising from a coffee tin over three candles (in a safety tray on the floor) to a 'cold water tank' on a stool and thence flowing back to the 'boiler'. The popular experiment that had helped them most in discovering how to do this had been the lowering of a bottle of hot blue water into a basin of cold water with the consequent rising of a streak of blue through the clear cold water. They had also seen how a stain of ink can be made to circulate in a tank of water where one end is cooled and the other end is heated.

Solenoid
(right) testing
(below) opening garage door.

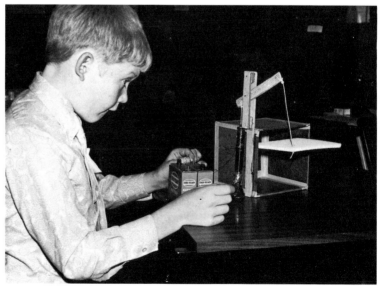

138

Once they had learned these things work began intensively on the house. They fitted a lighting circuit to the house and powered it by a 2-volt battery. Then they hung their newly made wallpaper and the curtains that they had printed. The tilers talked more and more volubly in geometrical terms as they compared their tiling patterns on the triangle-covered and hexagon-covered floors. They stuck the tiles firmly to the false floor and fitted it into the house.

By this time inter-group visiting was increasing and so learning was becoming more general. Intensive writing, unsolicited, was becoming prolific. Children had given the house a name and address and were writing letters to one another at this address and to their own homes from this address. Some children broke into poetry about the house. Certainly most children had a general idea about what all had discovered.

Soon the central heating system was fitted, with plastic pipes (as used for windscreen washers) running from a 'boiler' behind the house, through the rooms, to a tank on the still flat roof and so back to the boiler. Work was under way to construct, with geometrical accuracy, eaves for the ultimate roofing of the house. It interested us that children rejected a shallower isoceles triangle for the eaves, seeming to find more security in the equilateral one. Ultimately, they roofed the house with carefully measured roofing felt. Concurrently others 'glazed' the windows with thin Perspex, hinged the front door to the house and tiled the ceilings with square polystyrene tiles. By this time, as they rested from their labours, many were delving into books

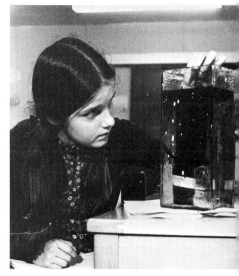

Blue hot water rising through cold clear water.

The boiler for the house.

Equilateral triangle work on eaves.

about houses in other lands and houses in history and in literature and in poetry.

Throughout the whole project individual children had kept simple time sheets of their own (a) learning time, and (b) 'qualified' working time at their 'trades'. Two boys telephoned the labour exchange (who had been warned in advance) and asked the hourly rates for each trade. All then estimated what they would have earned on a real building site. Not one child considered it was enough.

Towards the end of the project the classroom was a seething mass of purposeful activity. Working groups had generally broken into mere partnerships.

How does all this illustrate the developmental psychology taught us by Piaget?

As in the Stonehenge project, the chief application of Piagetian principles lay in the plentiful experience in 'concrete reasoning' that the experiments provided. In this instance most of the ideas involved were scientific and mathematical ones. From the point of view of developmental psychology very much the same mental activity is involved in both subject areas, i.e. the application of basic concepts plus intermediate stages of the skills of implication, negation, reciprocation and so forth, in empirically attempted experiments on materials. Frequent experiences of this sort, with materials, prepare the child for the abstract reasoning he will begin to be able to achieve in adolescence.

The house.

140

Books by Jean Piaget

published by Routledge & Kegan Paul Ltd, London:

The Child's Conception of Number (with A. Szeminska), 1952 (U.S. Humanities Press Inc.).

The Child's Conception of Physical Causality, 1930 (U.S. Humanities Press Inc.).

The Child's Conception of Time, 1970 (U.S. Basic Books Inc.).

The Child's Conception of Movement and Speed, 1970 (U.S. Humanities Press Inc.).

The Child's Conception of the World, 1929 (U.S. Humanities Press Inc.).

The Child's Construction of Reality, 1955 (U.S. and Canada: Basic Books Inc.).

Insights and Illusions of Philosophy, 1972 (U.S. and Canada: World Publishing Co.).

Judgement and Reasoning in the Child, 1928 (U.S. Humanities Press Inc.).

The Language and Thought of the Child, 1926 (U.S. Humanities Press Inc.).

The Mechanisms of Perception, 1969 (U.S. Basic Books Inc.).

The Moral Judgement of the Child, 1932 (U.S. Free Press).

The Origin of Intelligence in the Child, 1953 (U.S. International Universities Press).

Play, Dreams and Imitation in Childhood, 1951 (U.S. W.W. Norton & Co. Inc.).

The Principles of Genetic Epistemology, 1972 (U.S. Basic Books Inc.).

The Psychology of Intelligence, 1950 (U.S. Routledge & Kegan Paul).

Structuralism, 1971 (U.S. Basic Books Inc.).

With Bärbel Inhelder
The Child's Conception of Geometry (with A. Szeminska), 1960 (U.S. Basic Books Inc.).

The Child's Conception of Space, 1956 (U.S. Humanities Press Inc.).

The Early Growth of Logic in the Child: Classification and Seriation, 1964 (U.S. Harper & Row).

The Growth of Logical Thinking From Childhood to Adolescence, 1958 (U.S. and Canada: Basic Books Inc.).

Mental Imagery in the Child, 1970 (U.S. Basic Books Inc.).

The Psychology of the Child, 1969 (U.S. and Canada: Basic Books Inc.).

With Paul Fraisse
Experimental Psychology: Its Scope and Method (9 vols.), vol. 1 (1968), vol. 4 (1970), vol. 5 (1968), vol. 7 (1969) (U.S. Basic Books Inc.).

Index